California Government and Politics Today

California Government and Politics Today

NINTH EDITION

Mona Field
Glendale Community College

Charles P. Sohner
El Camino College, Emeritus

New York San Francisco Boston
London Toronto Sydney Tokyo Singapore Madrid
Mexico City Munich Paris Cape Town Hong Kong Montreal

Publisher: Priscilla McGeehon
Senior Acquisitions Editor : Eric Stano
Associate Editor: Anita Castro
Marketing Manager: Megan Galvin-Fak
Production Manager: Ellen MacElree
Project Coordination, Text Design, and Electronic Page Makeup: Electronic Publishing Services Inc., NYC
Cover Designer/Manager: John Callahan
Cover Photo: PhotoDisc, Inc.
Manufacturing Buyer: Lucy Hebard
Printer and Binder: The Maple-Vail Book Manufacturing Group
Cover Printer: John P. Pow

Library of Congress Cataloging-in Publication Data

Field, Mona.
California government and politics today / Mona Field, Charles P. Sohner.—9th ed.
p. cm.
Includes bibliographical references and index.
ISBN 0-321-07998-1
1. California—Politics and government—1951– I. Sohner, Charles P. II. Title.
JK8716.F54 2001
320.9794—dc21 00-067388
CIP

Please visit our website at http://www.ablongman.com

ISBN 0-321-07998-1

3 4 5 6 7 8 9 10—MA—04 03 02

Dedication

*To my colleague, friend,
and mentor, Charles
P. Sohner, with immense
gratitude for the
opportunity to continue the
educational and social
vision this book represents.*

MONA FIELD

Contents

Preface

Since the earliest explorers and conquistadores, California has held a mystique of golden potential for people from all over the world. Today's California is a reflection of its own past as well as a complex, ever-changing mosaic of the future. It is a destination for people from around the world, including the other forty-nine states. California today is a "salad bowl" of ethnicities, classes, and cultures, all of whom must coexist despite their many differences.

It is this text's goal to present the complexity not only of the political process but also of the social and economic circumstances in California today. The concise (yet thorough) exploration of these themes is designed to give readers many opportunities to reflect on their experiences living here and to consider ways in which they can become part of the process.

Features which make the text accessible to readers include opening quotations for each chapter, charts and maps, appendices which include a fully expanded glossary (defining each word that appears in italics in the text), a list of useful websites, a page dedicated to how to get in touch with your elected officials, and a list of political organizations accessible to students. In addition, each chapter closes with "Questions to Consider," designed to help readers evaluate the material through their own personal reflections and critical thinking. Students can also use the Study Guide available through their instructors; this guide enables students to answer questions as they read.

Special emphases of this edition that add to its currency are issues relating to numerous ballots initiatives that the courts are evaluating, the long-awaited turnaround in the state's economy, the continuing increase in population as well as in social and cultural diversity, and the expansion of the electorate to include new citizens eager to vote. As always, the book pays close attention to the demographic and economic indicators and the political implications thereof. For the benefit of instructors, an Instructor's Manual with Tests is available from your Allyn & Bacon/Longman sales representative.

The authors' highest aim is to enlighten and inform the readers while gently reminding them that the fate of our golden state is in our hands. If we do not participate, who will? We hope our efforts are successful, and we thank those who made this book possible: our editor, Eric Stano; our reviewers, Elena V. Dorabji at San Jose State University and Edgar Kaskla at California State University, Long Beach, whose critiques guided this revision; and, of course, our families, who understand our periodic disappearances into our offices.

We remain fully responsible for our work, both the positive aspects and any omissions or errors which it may contain.

Please read, reflect, and consider joining us in a long-term commitment to make California the very best it can be.

Mona Field

Charles P. Sohner

CHAPTER 1

California Politics in Perspective

"California, after all, is special, a nonstop preview of the future, the cutting edge of the trend that will overtake the country—for good or for ill"

Susan F. Rasky, University of California, Berkeley, School of Journalism

"Never a dull moment" could be the California motto as the twenty-first century dawns. After several very tough years in the early 1990s, the economy finally recovered from the recession caused largely by the end of the Cold War and the loss of over 500,000 defense related jobs. By the year 2000, California was booming with new and revived industries, including high-tech, biomedical, entertainment, telecommunications and tourism. Yet just as tax revenues were pouring in and plans being made to improve long-neglected public schools, the "energy crisis" struck. The state's political leaders panicked and the public fumed over high rates, blackouts and taxpayer bailouts of utility corporations.

Assuming some longterm resolution, California hopes to recover from the crisis and retain its status as number one in agricultural production[1] as well as in import-export traffic at its Long Beach and San Pedro ports.[2] If California were a separate nation, it would rank eighth in the world in Gross Domestic Production. California still leads the nation in population, with hints that by the year 2010 the state will be home to about 37 million Americans, of whom more than half will be "minorities." California's influence on the national scene will continue to be enormous, and individual Californians with the right education and skills will continue to do very well. Those who benefit from the good times are earning higher salaries and paying more taxes, allowing politicians to spend more money on essential public services while also reducing vehicle license fees and admission to state parks. A strong economy allows many Californians to do well, and permits the state to provide better services. But even during economics booms, not every individual's financial circumstances improve. California ranks fifth in the nation in growing income inequality, and the average working family has actually lost income over the past twenty years.[3]

California's status as a *two-tier* state, in which those without adequate education remain caught in low-wage, no-benefits jobs, remains one of the state's biggest challenges. Improving education is a major theme of politicians such as Governor Gray Davis, who vowed not to run for a second term if the state's school children did not improve their academic test scores. Despite improved funding to schools, urban public schools frequently lack decent restrooms, much less adequate textbooks, laboratories, or libraries.

National Impact: Setting Trends for the Country

In the year 2000, California celebrated its *sesquicentennial* (150th anniversary of statehood) as perhaps the most powerful state in the nation. Since national political power is linked directly to population, and because California has remained the most populous state for several decades, California maintains its enormous clout in the national scene. The state has 53 of the 435 members of the House of Representatives, more than any other state, and 55 *electoral votes*, more than a fifth of the 270 necessary to elect a president.

California's national importance flows largely from three traditional sources of political power—money, publicity, and population. Even during the prolonged economic slump of the early 1990s, California remained the home of one-fifth of the nation's wealthiest people.[4] Although the rich are a tiny minority of the population, they can have enormous influence on politics, both through campaign contributions and through their own political activism. Wealthy individuals with political agendas can come from "nowhere" to win elections (such as former Los Angeles Mayor Richard Riordan) or can use their dollars to create and subsidize ballot propositions (such as Ron Unz's multimillion-dollar investment in Prop. 227 to end bilingual education).

Along with dollars, media and publicity also play a key role in political outcomes. During both good times and bad, California gets an ample share of attention in the national media. The state still gets international media coverage for happy events such as the annual Tournament of Roses Parade, as well as less favorable attention when its residents suffer the ravages of earthquakes or major fires. Because California is home to people from all over the world, events in Los Angeles or San Francisco may be front-page news in Manila, Ho Chi Minh City, Seoul, Hong Kong, or San Salvador.

It is sheer numbers, however, that contribute most to California's political might. Its 34 million people[5] earn the state both the largest congressional delegation and the largest bloc of electoral votes, and also, under most circumstances, enable it to receive more federal grants and government contracts than almost any other state. For the 2000 Census, state officials worked with federal Census staff to publicize the importance of being counted, by reminding Californians that population count determines how much federal funding comes to the state. With the numerical advantages

TABLE 1.1

California's Population: Growth Since Statehood

Year	*Population*
1850	92,597
1860	379,994
1870	560,247
1880	864,694
1890	1,213,398
1900	1,485,053
1910	2,377,549
1920	3,426,861
1930	5,677,251
1940	6,907,387
1950	10,586,223
1960	15,717,204
1970	19,971,069
1980	23,667,902
1990	31,400,000
1997	32,609,000
Projected 2005	38,200,000

Source: U.S. Census Bureau, State Department of Finance.

of California's ever-growing population (see Table 1.1), it is no surprise that presidential candidates often visit California more times than any other state as they campaign for those electoral votes, and it is no wonder that high-level California politicians are often mentioned as future presidential contenders.

The State and Its People: Power Blocs in Conflict

Despite California's prominence in national affairs, the daily lives of its people are affected more closely by the politics of their own state. The state determines the grounds for divorce, the traffic regulations, public college tuition fees, penalties for drug possession, and the qualifications one needs to become a barber, psychologist, or lawyer. It establishes the amount of unemployment compensation, the location of highways, the subjects to be taught in school, and the rates to be charged by telephone, gas, and electric companies. Along with the local governments under its control, it regulates building construction, provides police and fire protection, and spends about 15 percent of the total value of goods and services produced by California residents.

The policy decisions made in these and other areas are influenced by the distribution of political power among various groups with competing needs and aspirations. Some of the power blocs reflect the same conflicts of interest that the nation experiences: labor vs. business; landlords vs. tenants; environmentalists vs. oil companies. But, as in so many things, these battles are fought on a grander scale in California. With its incredibly complex array of local governments, including over 6,000 *special districts* to provide everything from street lights to public education, California's political system almost defies understanding. No wonder that voters have shown their overall mistrust of elected officials and turned to *ballot initiatives* to make new laws and even to amend the state constitution.

These ballot initiatives, or *propositions*, deal with everything from juvenile crime to "limit on marriage," from Indian gaming rights to the ever-present insurance industry issues. While political experts despise the use of initiatives to set public policy, well-organized and profitable petition-gathering companies continue to persuade voters to sign their names in order to place these items on the ballot. The outcome of these initiative battles usually depends on such factors as money, media, and the public mood.

The State and the Federal System: A Complex Relationship

Like the other states, California is part of the American federal system. *Federalism* distributes power to both the national and state governments, thereby creating a system of dual citizenship and authority. It is a complex arrangement designed to assure the unity of the country while at the same time permitting the states to reflect the diversity of their people and economies. Although national and state authority overlap in such areas as taxation and highway construction (examples of what are known as concurrent powers), each level of government also has its own policy domain. The U.S. Constitution gives the national government its powers, including such areas as immigration law, interstate commerce, foreign policy, national defense, and international relations. The states are permitted to do anything that is not prohibited or that the Constitution does not assign to the national government.

Within each state, the distribution of powers is *unitary*. This means that the cities, counties, and other units of local government get their authority from the state. States and their local bodies generally focus their powers on such services as education, public safety, and health and welfare.

Just as California has a mighty impact on the country as a whole, the national government exerts reciprocal influence on the states. Federal funds often come with strings attached. Los Angeles County received a federal *bailout* worth $1 billion to avoid a closure of its health care system for the uninsured, but had to beg for a waiver of federal rules in order to receive the money. Such federal *mandates* continue to cause debate over *states' rights* and the proper role of the federal government, with recent trends suggesting that *devolution*, or the passing of authority from federal to state and local governments, will continue.

However, federal funds do not always come directly to government itself. For nearly fifty years, between World War II and the end of the Cold

War, California's private defense industry relied heavily on federal contracts to create a thriving military-based economy. Major corporations, such as Lockheed, Hughes, Rockwell, and many others, enjoyed high profits and provided well-paying, secure jobs to engineers, managers, secretaries, and assembly-line workers. When the Cold War ended in 1989, this entire military contract system suddenly downsized and many military bases closed, leaving a huge hole in the California economy. Fortunately, in recent years many of the defense-related companies have transformed themselves into high-tech businesses,[6] while many former military bases are being retrofitted to serve as parks and shelters for the homeless.[7] Retraining, education, and job creation continue to be themes for California as it recovers from its longtime dependence on the federal defense budget.

While relations between the federal government and each state are complex and significant, the relations between states are also important. The U.S. Constitution requires every state to honor the laws of every other state, so that marriages and other contracts made in one state are respected in all states and criminals trying to escape justice cannot find safe haven by leaving the state in which they have been convicted. This federal requirement has caused considerable political activity regarding gay marriage rights since Vermont has created a civil union for gays that may be upheld in California despite the voters' strong support for Prop. 22 (2000), which denied the right to gay "marriage" in the state.

Federalism is perhaps America's greatest political invention. It permits states to enact their diverse policy preferences into law on such matters as gambling, prostitution, trash disposal, and wilderness protection, and thus encourages experiments that may spread to other states. California has become known as a place of experimentation, and these new political ideas often spread across the nation. *Conservative* themes such as tax revolts, anti-immigration sentiments, and the backlash against affirmative action all began as successful ballot propositions in California, while *liberal* ideas such as legalization of marijuana for medical purposes and government-provided health care for all also have become ballot battles.

Because federalism allows states great autonomy, and because California has developed a complex web of local governments, the average California voter must make numerous decisions at the polls. Each Californian, whether a U.S. citizen or not, lives in a number of election jurisdictions, including a congressional district, a state Senate district, an Assembly district, and a county Supervisorial district, plus (in most cases) a city, a school district, and a community college district. (See Figure 1.1.) This array of political jurisdictions provides many opportunities to exercise democracy. It also creates confusion, overlaps, and many occasions on which voters feel unable to evaluate fully the qualifications of candidates or the merits of ballot propositions.

Other problems linked to federalism include outdated state boundaries that have created some "super-states," with land masses and populations that may be ungovernable, and the differences in resources between states. California's size has certainly caused numerous contro-

Partisan Offices			
National Level	**Elected by**	**Term**	**Election Year**
President	Entire state	4 years	Years divisible by four
U.S. Senators	Entire state	6 years	Every six years counting from 1992 Every six years counting from 1994
Members of Congress	Districts	2 years	Even-numbered years
State Level			
Governor[1] Lt. Governor[1] Secretary of State[1] Controller[1] Treasurer[1] Attorney General[1] Insurance Commissioner	Entire state	4 years	Even-numbered years when there is no presidential election
Members of Board of Equalization[1]	Districts	4 years	Same as governor
State Senators[1]	Districts	4 years	Same as governor for even-numbered districts Same as president for odd-numbered districts
Assembly members[2]	Districts	2 years	Even-numbered years
Nonpartisan Offices			
State Level			
Superintendent of Public Instruction	Entire state	4 years	Same as governor
Supreme Court justices	Entire state	12 years	Same as governor
Court of Appeal justices	Entire state	12 years	Same as governor
Superior Court judges	Counties	6 years	Even-numbered years

[1]Limited to two terms by Proposition 140
[2]Limited to three terms by Proposition 140

FIGURE 1.1 Federal and State Officials Elected by California Voters
Source: League of Women Voters.

versies over whether the state should be divided somehow. Meanwhile, variations in states' resources perpetuate inequality in schools, public hospitals, and other government facilities at a time when the nation as a whole is concerned about how to provide these services. The federal system also promotes rivalry between states as they compete to attract new businesses (and jobs) or keep existing ones. Among the tactics used in this struggle are tax breaks, reduced worker compensation, and relaxed environmental protection standards. What remains of California's military–industrial complex, such as Boeing and Lockheed's "Aerospace Valley," must compete for federal contracts against sophisticated efforts from Texas and Missouri.[8] On the larger international scale, the North American Free Trade Agreement (NAFTA) has enhanced the appeal of relocating across the border to Mexico, because goods produced by low-wage labor in Mexican *maquiladoras* can enter the United States with no import tariffs. In the global economy of the new millennium, California faces tremendous challenges in providing decent jobs, education, health services, and, in general, the high quality of life that the state has always promoted as its chief claim to fame.

Questions to Consider

Using Your Text and Your Own Experiences

1. What are some of the pros and cons of life in California? Do these depend in part on whether you live in a rural or an urban area?
2. What are some of the challenges facing the state as it enters the new millennium? What can elected officials do to resolve these challenges? How do you fit into the challenges facing our state?
3. Take a class survey. How many students were born in California? How many are immigrants, either from another state or another nation? Team up so that an "immigrant" is paired with a "native" Californian. Teams or pairs can discuss the different experiences of those born here vs. those who immigrated.

Notes

1. Dave Lesher, "Officials Crow About State's Farm Economy," *Los Angeles Times,* 17 July 1997, p. A3.
2. James Flanigan, "Ports' Growth Bodes Well for Labor Talks," *Los Angeles Times,* 23 June 1999, p. C1.
3. "Legislative Conference Focuses on Wage Gap," *California Labor News,* California Labor Federation, April 2000, p. 1.
4. "Bill Gates Tops List in Forbes Ranking of Richest in U.S.," *Los Angeles Times,* 3 October 1994, p. D1.
5. Hans P. Johnson, "How Many Californians? A Review of Population Projections for the State," *California Counts,* Public Policy Institute of California, Vol. 1, No. 1, October 1999, p. 1.
6. Ashley Dunn, "Area's High-Tech Firms Outgrow Military Origins," *Los Angeles Times,* 11 March 2000, p. A1.
7. Queena Sook Kim, "Homeless Find Good Life on Former Base," *Los Angeles Times,* 17 April 2000, p. A3.
8. Andrew Blankstein, "California Joins Fray to Keep Aerospace Alive and Here," *Los Angeles Times,* 28 March 2000, p. A1.

CHAPTER 2

The Californians: Land, People, and Political Culture

"There will always be a California dream ... but it won't come with mere wishing.... we must all become 'dreamers of the day,' exploring the future with eyes and hearts wide open."

A. G. Block, journalist

The political process in California, as in other states, is conditioned by many geographic, *demographic*, and cultural influences. While geography changes only slowly, population shifts and cultural influences can rather suddenly inject new and unpredictable threads into the complex web that forms the state's identity and future prospects.

Geographic Influences: Where Are We?

With an area of 156,000 square miles, California is larger than Italy, Japan, or England and is the third-largest state, following Alaska and Texas. It is shaped like a gigantic stocking, with a length more than twice its width. If California were superimposed on the East Coast, it would cover six states, from Florida to New York.[1] The enormity of the state as well as recurrent battles over water supplies and financial resources have resulted in periodic proposals that the state be divided into two or even three separate states, with the presumption that the northern, central, and southern regions could each stand alone as political entities.[2]

While California's size has contributed to its political dynamics, its location has been at least as important. As the leading state on what is called the Pacific Rim (those states bordering the Pacific Ocean and facing the Far East), California is already the nation's number one exporter, with potential for even greater growth as mainland China's entry into full trading status expands the state's export markets.[3] California is also one of only fifteen states that borders a foreign nation. In part as a result of its proximity to Mexico, Californians of Mexican descent have become the largest ethnic group in the state, one which includes both first-generation Mexican immigrants and "Chicanos," whose parents or ancestors originally came from that country.

Two other geographic influences command attention: rich natural resources and spectacularly beautiful terrain. Between the majestic Sierra Nevada range along the eastern border and the Coastal Mountains on the west lies the Central Valley—one of the richest agricultural regions in the world. As a result, California leads the nation in farm output, although agriculture's political influence has diminished as agricultural lands have been developed into housing tracts and shopping centers.[4] While over 40 percent of the state is forested, battles over environmental standards and redwood preservation have somewhat reduced the power of the lumber industry and caused lengthy litigation.[5] California has plentiful oil, yet even the once-invincible petroleum industry has occasionally been prevented from building pipelines through urban areas by *grassroots* organizations concerned about safety. While agriculture, timber, and oil remain economically important as well as environmentally controversial, another natural resource is also the subject of continual political debate over how much to exploit it: California's landscape. Ranging across arid deserts, a thousand-mile shoreline, and remote mountain wilderness, the terrain itself is a continuing battlefield between conservationists and commercial recreation developers. Much of California is owned by the public, with forty-three national parks, forests, recreation areas, and monuments, plus the state's own vast acreage of public forests, parks, and beaches. Despite the huge expanses of undeveloped land, Californians are a largely urban people, with over 80 percent living in cities.[6]

Demographic Influences: Who Are We?

After a few slow years during the *recession* of the early 1990s, California has once again returned to its historical pattern of rapid population growth. The number of Californians continues to increase as a result of both birth rates and immigration, while continuing medical advances will keep death rates low as the senior population grows to record-breaking numbers.[7] Long-term predictions suggest that the state will have nearly 50 million people by the year 2025, creating enormous challenges regarding housing, education, health care, transportation, water supplies, and environmental quality. Demographers predict that California will remain the most populous state, with over 12 percent of the nation's people.[8]

California continues to be the most diverse state, with residents from virtually every nation and ethnic group on the planet. For the foreseeable future, there will be no one "majority" group, but by 2005, Latinos, Asian-Americans and African-Americans will combine to form a numerical "minority" majority.[9] Figure 2.1 breaks down the workforce by ethnic

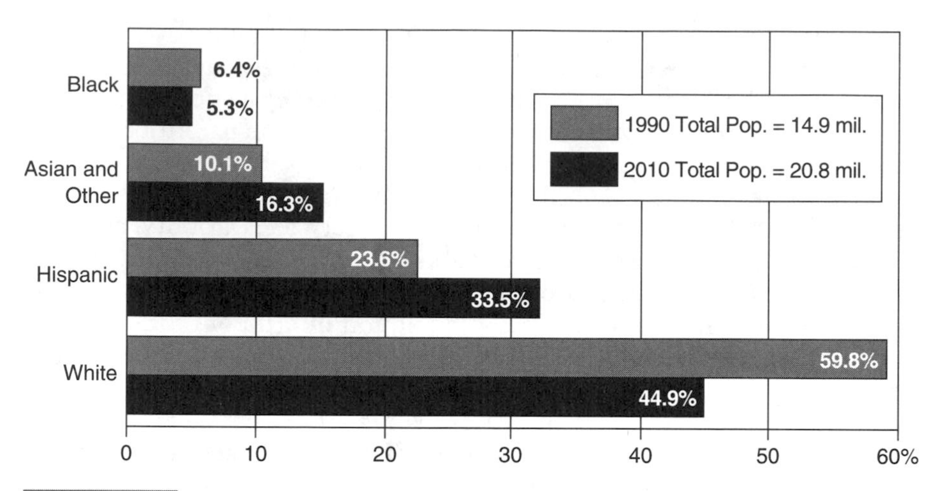

FIGURE 2.1 California Labor Force by Ethnic Group, 1990–2010: Percentage of Labor Force Population

Source: Center for Continuing Study of the California Economy.

group. International immigration to California will continue, with California receiving about one-fourth of all immigrants to the United States,[10] while "American immigrants" from other states will continue to find the California lifestyle appealing. Due in large part to economic prosperity, the anti-immigrant scapegoating of the early 1990s has given way to increased public interest in intercultural cooperation, as evidenced by numerous government-sponsored multicultural festivities and awareness events.

Californians generally seem to realize that the increasing racial and ethnic diversity of the state's population is unlikely to change. Many of the foreign immigrants come from Mexico, Central America, and the Asian Pacific region, with substantial numbers arriving from Russia, the Middle East, and the Caribbean.[11] Unlike their predecessors of other eras, recent immigrants do not necessarily settle in urban areas, but are increasingly integrating formerly "white" suburbs such as Santa Clarita and parts of Orange County.[12] As immigrants *assimilate* into California's culture, they can choose whether to move from legal residency to full citizenship, and thus gain the privilege to vote. Due to changes in federal law as well as fears created by the passage of Prop. 187 (a largely unconstitutional 1994 measure which attempted to impose state laws regarding immigration), the desire of many legal residents to become citizens has created large backlogs in the federal Immigration and Naturalization Service (INS) system.

Whether they are citizens or residents, concentrations of immigrant ethnic groups have already altered the social and political landscape in many California communities. Out of choice or necessity, ethnic enclaves develop wherever a group puts down roots, their presence reflected in the language of storefront signs, distinctive architecture, and types of food available. Daly City is called "Little Manila," and Fresno is home to 30,000 Hmong, members of a Laotian hill tribe. Stockton has 35,000 refugees from several areas of Indochina; Glendale has a substantial concentration of Armenians; Westminster, in Orange County, is known as "Little Saigon," and Monterey Park, the first city in the continental United States with an Asian majority,[13] is 56 percent Chinese. About 3 million Hispanics, mostly Mexican, live in Los Angeles County, and the school children there speak 80 different languages.[14]

Since immigration to California continues at a high rate, American-born ethnic minorities are often mistakenly lumped into the same categories as the newcomers. Because they have the same ethnic heritage as their immigrant relatives, American-born Latinos and Asians may be subject to similar prejudices and discrimination. Despite being U.S. citizens, many Latinos still face enormous obstacles in achieving adequate educations, while Asian-Americans have often been stereotyped into "perfect student" roles that place burdens on those who do not fulfill that expectation. Recent studies show that newly arrived immigrant youth have the highest appreciation for education, while second-generation American minorities show signs of losing faith in their ability to achieve the California dream through hard work.[15] (See Table 2.1.) This may suggest that *acculturation* is a mixed blessing for immigrant children. Meanwhile, African-Americans, the third largest ethnic minority group, continue to see their numbers decline in proportion to the fast-growing Latino and

TABLE 2.1

Ranking of Average Income Among 30-Year-Old California Workers (Overall Average $32,861)

Category	*Income*
White males	$39,279
Asian male citizens	$35,361
Hispanic male citizens	$34,554
Black males	$30,842
White females	$28,938
Asian female citizens	$28,046
Black females	$26,588
Hispanic female citizens	$25,488
Asian male immigrants	$24,713
Hispanic male immigrants	$21,191
Hispanic female immigrants	$19,392
Asian female immigrants	$19,202

Source: McLeod, Ramon G. "White Women, Young Minorities Make Pay Gains," *San Francisco Chronicle*, 6 September 1993, p. 13.

Asian communities, with resulting concerns about how blacks can compete successfully for educational and political opportunities while other ethnic groups begin to dominate numerically.

Population diversity, of course, embraces far more than ethnicity. Collectively, Californians seem to embody virtually the whole range of religious beliefs, including nearly 20 percent who profess no religion at all. No "majority religion" exists in California, with 45 percent Protestant, 25 percent Roman Catholic, 5 percent Jewish, and 7 percent "other." About one-third of Californians claim to be "born-again Christians," which may partially account for the strength of the Christian Coalition, a political movement based on a belief that fundamentalist Christian theology should guide American politics.[16]

Another of California's diverse groupings is the gay community, often a target of the Christian Coalition. The most recent example of this battle was the passage of Prop. 22, sponsored by the fundamentalist Christian organizations as a statement against gay marriage. The well-financed campaign of the churches easily defeated gay and civil rights opponents. Despite that electoral defeat, recent opinion polls indicate that over 80 percent of Californians oppose discrimination on the basis of sexual orientation,[17] and gay and lesbian political leaders and their allies continue to fight *homophobia* and advocate for equal rights and freedoms for gay, lesbian, bisexual, and transgender Californians.

California's Political Culture: How We Think

Each state has a distinctive political style that is shaped not only by its geography and population characteristics but also by the values and attitudes shared by most of its people. These elements constitute what is sometimes called the political culture. In many ways, California is similar to that of the rest of the country and is conditioned by the same influences. Californians embrace the principles of patriotism, capitalism, and democracy as fervently as any Americans. But there are differences as well, stemming from both unique historical development and the steady emergence of distinctive problems demanding political attention. California's frontier heritage, for example, includes a legacy of materialistic individualism that may exceed that of most other states.

Perhaps this focus on the freedom to cash in and acquire the status symbols of California life (a pool, a Porsche, and a private school for the kids) has made California more of a *two-tier* state than some others. Inequality in household incomes continues to challenge state leaders, with the major cause being the decline in income of those at the bottom. At the low end, the poorest working families earn 22 percent less in inflation-adjusted dollars than they did in 1969,[18] and even the middle class feels squeezed by the high cost of housing, child care, and health care.[19] Those aware of these facts no doubt cheered the successful janitors' strike in Los Angeles, which made clear how low-wage workers enable the high-income white-collar class to arrive to clean offices daily. A reinvigorated labor movement may be one of the ways that the income gap is reduced in future years.

Aggravating the gaps between rich and poor is the high cost of housing,[20] inadequate health care for the one-fifth of Californians who are uninsured, and the increasing competition for higher-education opportunities. However, the booming economy has allowed some improvements in recent years. After nearly twenty years of declining resources, California's public schools have received new funds, while community colleges and state universities are holding tuition costs down. Local governments are attempting to tackle the need for low- and moderate-cost housing. Employment rates are excellent, with much of the growth in well-paying, high-tech and entertainment jobs.

With this mix of economic good news and bad news, and the sense that the haves are doing much better than the have-nots, California's political climate is also mixed. After years of low voter turnout, the state may be seeing a slight increase in voting among certain groups. The *electorate*, which had been nearly 80 percent white, has seen a 37 percent increase in Latino voter participation, many of whom are newly *naturalized* citizens eager to vote against politicians and ballot measures that insult immigrants or ethnic communities. Yet overall voter turnout remains too low for real democracy to prevail. One possible solution may occur if local experiments in online voting result in statewide elections becoming available via the Internet.[21]

For some Californians, the recognition of government's power motivates them not only to vote but also to form political associations to represent their views. Because of the ethnic, socioeconomic, and cultural diversity of the state, California is home to a wide variety of political organizations. The ideologies behind the organizations can be simplistically summarized by the traditional labels of American politics: conservative and liberal. The *conservative* side of California politics is torn between those who support maximum freedom for both business and individuals and those who like free enterprise but prefer government to regulate personal behavior such as sexuality and abortion. These uneasy partners form the basis of the California Republican Party, and their areas of agreement often end with tax cuts and calls to *privatize* government services. Moderate Republicans, especially women, often feel stuck between their views on economic matters and their party's continuing domination by "cultural conservatives," who promote an antichoice, antigay and antifeminist agenda. It is these moderate Republicans, along with the many independent voters, who have helped turn California into a Democratic-controlled state by voting Democrats into a majority position in both the executive and legislative branches of state government.

On the other side of the political spectrum, the *liberal* movement in California has moved considerably to the center. One-time genuine *left-wing* ideas, such as promoting social equality and government action to solve problems, are now modified to meet the demands of a competitive global economy. Yet some of the idealism of California's famous 1960s activists has lived on, as some of the same individuals who fought for free speech and civil rights at the University of California at Berkeley forty years ago are now elected officials, nearly all Democrats. Many Californians are uninterested in traditional political labels, and, in the noble American pragmatic tradition, just want to solve problems. Perhaps this practical attitude and a reduction in fervent ideologies will help the state move forward successfully into the new millennium. The state is full of California dreamers, both those who have achieved their goals and those still working toward their dreams.

Questions to Consider

Using Your Text and Your Own Experiences

1. What is the relationship between California's geography (size, location, topography, etc.) and its economic and political situation?
2. What are some of the pros and cons of the state's ethnic diversity?
3. Discuss the issue of social and economic inequality. What problems are caused by the vast gaps between rich and poor? Are there any advantages to having a two-tier society?

Notes

1. *Los Angeles Times,* December 17, 1987, part I, p. 3.
2. Charles Price, "The Longshot Bid to Split California," *California Government and Politics Annual,* 1994–94, p. 10.
3. California Trade and Commerce Agency, "California Exports: 1999," http://commerce.ca.gov/international/facts/1999.html
4. "Competition for Land," *American Farmland,* American Farmland Trust, Fall 1996, p. 5.
5. John Skow, "Redwoods: The Last Stand," *Time,* 6 June 1994, p. 58.
6. "81% of Californians Live in Cities, State Agency Says," *Los Angeles Times,* 5 May 1999, p. A38.
7. Faye Fiore, "Population Surge of 18 Million Seen for State by 2025," *Los Angeles Times,* 25 August 1997, p. A1.
8. Hans P. Johnson, "How Many Californians? A Review of Population Projections for the State," *California Counts,* Public Policy Institute of California, Vol. 1, No. 1, October 1999, p. 1.
9. Armando Acuna, "Changes in State's Ethnic Balance are Accelerating," *Los Angeles Times,* 20 October 1999, p. A3.
10. Patrick J. McDonnell, "1990s on Track to Set a Record for Immigration," *Los Angeles Times,* 24 January 1999, p. A10.
11. Julia Franco, "The Great Divide: Immigration in the 1990s," *Los Angeles Times,* 14 November 1993, p. A1.
12. Susan Goldsmith, "Immigrants Find American Dream in Suburbs," *Los Angeles Daily News,* June 12, 1994, p. 3.

13. Seth Mydans, "Asian Investors Create a Pocket of Prosperity," *New York Times,* 17 October 1994, p. A8.
14. *The Economist,* 13 October 1990, pp. 8–10.
15. Elaine Woo, "Immigrants, U.S. Peers Differ Starkly on Schools," *Los Angeles Times,* 22 February 1996, p. A1.
16. Mark Nollinger, "The New Crusaders: The Christian Right Storms California's Political Bastions," *California Journal,* January 1993, p. 6.
17. Jennifer Warren, "Gays Gaining Acceptance in State, Poll Finds," *Los Angeles Times,* 14 June 2000, p. A3.
18. Mark Arax, Mary Curtius, and Soraya Sarhaddi Nelson, "California Income Gap Grows Amid Prosperity," *Los Angeles Times,* 9 January 2000, p. A1.
19. Dan Morain and Soraya Sarhaddi Nelson, "Problems of Middle-Income Families Studied," *Los Angeles Times,* 10 November 1999, p. A3.
20. Steven F. Hayward, "Preserving the American Dream: The Facts About Suburban Communities and Housing Choice," California Building Industry Association/Building Industry Institute, September 1996.
21. Eric Bailey, "'E-Voting' Urged as Way to Lift Turnout," *Los Angeles Times,* 17 January 2000, p. A3.

CHAPTER 3
California's Historical Development

"California will try to get by as it has always gotten by ... hoping that the regime of abundance will last forever, or at least for another generation."

James D. Houston, California scholar

California's modern history begins with the native population of about 300,000 people in approximately 100 linguistic/cultural "tribelets," who lived on this land before the Europeans arrived.[1] Despite the unique culture of each of the dozens of Native California tribes, very little information exists regarding the diverse groups which inhabited California during this period. Perhaps that is because these first Californians were so nearly exterminated. According to a New York newspaper in 1860, "in [other] States, the Indians have suffered wrongs and cruelties.... But history has no parallel to the recent atrocities perpetrated in California. Even the record of Spanish butcheries in Mexico and Peru has nothing so diabolical."[2] The hunter-gatherers of California were soon annihilated to make room for the *conquistadores*, whose desire for gold led them to murder and rape many of the people they found here.[3]

The Spanish Era: 1542–1822

In 1542, only fifty years after Columbus first came to the "New" World, Spain claimed California as a result of a voyage by Juan Rodriguez Cabrillo. More than two centuries passed, however, before the Spanish established their first colony. It was named San Diego and founded by an expedition headed by Gaspar de Portola, a military commander, and Junipero Serra, a missionary dedicated to converting the Indians to Roman Catholicism. Between 1769 and 1823, the Spanish conquerors built a series of missions running the length of California from San Diego to San Francisco, each with its own military post. By the time the missions were completed, most of the native cultures had been eradicated or severely distorted by the demands of Catholicism, and the *mestizo* residents of New Spain (which actually included most of Central America and Mexico as well as the U.S. Southwest) were ready to overthrow the Spanish colonial rulers and declare independence.

Mexican Dominance: 1821–1848

In 1821, Mexico declared itself free of Spanish rule. Soon after, the land now called California officially became part of the newly independent United States of Mexico. Civilian governments were established for the pueblos, or villages, but the distant government in Mexico City still viewed California as a remote and relatively unimportant colony. American settlers began to arrive in the 1840s, lured by the inviting climate and stories of economic opportunities. Many were imbued with the spirit of "*manifest destiny*," a belief that Americans had a mission to control the whole continent. When the United States failed in its attempt to buy California, it used a Texas boundary dispute as an excuse to launch the Mexican War in 1846. The war ended within a year, with the United States winning enormous lands including California, Arizona, New Mexico, and Texas, as well as large parts of Utah, Colorado, and Nevada. California came under American military rule, and in 1848 Mexico renounced its claims by signing the Treaty of Guadalupe Hidalgo, a document which promised the Mexican population of California that their language and property would be respected under the new government—a promise that was quickly broken. Within a short time, the ranchos of the *Californios* (those of Mexican descent) were grabbed by immigrants (Anglos), and much of these lands were later granted to the owners of the railroads.[4]

Americanization and Statehood: 1848–1850

The U.S. military occupation lasted three years. Congress, which normally places newly acquired lands under territorial government, was immobilized by a dispute over whether to permit slavery in its newest possession. Before the issue could be settled, gold was discovered in 1848, making California land the most highly prized in the entire world. In 1849, the year of the legendary "gold rush," the settlers adopted the first California constitution, largely pieced together from constitutional fragments adopted earlier by Iowa and New York. The Compromise of 1850, enacted by Congress, temporarily settled the slavery issue by admitting California as a free state, making it the thirty-first in the union and the first that did

FIGURE 3.1 **Map of California**

Source: Los Angeles County Almanac, 1991.

not border an existing state. (Figure 3.1 shows the county boundaries of California today.)

Today the legacy of the Spanish and Mexican periods can be found in California's architecture, place names, and food. But the character of state government is clearly based on Anglo-American traditions.

Consolidating Power: 1850–1902

During its first fifty years of statehood, California grew in both population and diversity. Newcomers from around the world came to seek their fortunes, and some were extraordinarily successful. Others, particularly during economic downturns, began to *scapegoat* less popular groups and call for their expulsion. Chinese immigrants, brought to this country to build the railroads cheaply, were major targets of overt racism and discrimination during the recession of the 1870s. Despite periods of decline, the overall economy boomed during this period, although the *Californios* generally became impoverished and forgotten as white Americans took charge. The economy shifted from mining to agriculture, and the arrival of the transcontinental railroad increased the frenzied population growth as well as the lust for power among those who owned the rails.

In 1879 the first state constitution was replaced by the one now in effect. In a preview of political events that seem to recur every time the state's economy sags, the second California constitution was loaded with anti-immigrant provisions (aimed at Asian immigrants) later declared invalid as violations of the U.S. Constitution.

The Progressive Legacy: 1902–1919

The *progressive movement* in California, like its national counterpart, arose at the beginning of the twentieth century. Its goal was to reduce the power of corrupt political parties and rich corporations which spent large sums to control politicians. In California, the primary target was the Southern Pacific Railroad, a corporation which owned one-fifth of all nonpublic land in the state. Its major stockholders—Charles Crocker, Leland Stanford, Collis P. Huntington, and Mark Hopkins—were the "Big Four" of state politics. According to their critics, they had bought "the best state legislature that money could buy."

Despite the power of the Big Four, the Progressives had remarkable success. Child labor laws and conservation policies were adopted. Political parties were weakened by imposing rigid legal controls on their internal organization and prohibiting candidates for city, county, education boards, and judicial office from revealing their party affiliation on the ballot. Today, all of these offices remain *nonpartisan*.

Possibly the most important legacies left by the Progressives were the *direct democracy* powers which permit voters to pass laws or amend the state constitution through the ballot box, as well as to recall elected officials from office through a special election.

The Twentieth Century, California Style

In the past century, California experienced many of the same major events as the rest of the nation: the Roaring Twenties, the Great Depression, the World War II economic boom. California's contributions to American history of these periods includes the near-election of a socialist governor in 1934 (and the *redbaiting* campaign to defeat him), the Depression-era migration of hundreds of thousands of people from the Midwest Dust Bowl to the "Golden State," and the continuing immigration of people lured by defense-industry jobs during World War II and the Cold War that followed. Throughout the century, through good and bad times, California's population continued to grow.

A long period of relative prosperity during the 1950s and 1960s never included everyone. When cheap labor was needed in the agricultural fields during World War II, Mexican *braceros* entered the country with temporary work permits, but were then expelled when their labor was no longer needed.[5] People of color experienced discrimination in housing, employment, and education. By the early 1960s, California's educational system was rocked by the street protests of UC Berkeley students protesting their own lack of free speech on campus as well as the unequal treatment of blacks in Bay Area businesses.[6] By the end of the 1960s, California was known as the center of a counterculture of drugs, antiwar sentiment, and sexual experimentation in places like San Francisco's Haight-Ashbury neighborhood.

During the *inflationary* period of the 1970s, Californians patiently sat in their cars waiting their turns to buy rationed gas at high prices and then voted their frustration with government by supporting the deep property tax cuts of Prop. 13 (1978). By the 1980s, former California Governor Ronald Reagan was President and the economy again boomed, although the promised "trickle-down" of economic improvements to the poor did not occur. The century ended with a decade of change: the *recession* of the early 1990s with its inevitable cuts in public services, the anger at politicians expressed by voter-approved *term limits* (Prop. 140; 1990), and the explosion of Latino participation in politics by the end of the century. With most Latinos identifying with the Democratic Party, California begins the new millennium with Democrats holding a majority in both houses of the legislature as well as Democrat Gray Davis in the governor's seat.

California's Constitution: A Few Highlights

Like the national government, the California political system is characterized by a separation of powers, freedom, and democracy. Certain differences, however, deserve attention. Although the separation of powers involves the traditional three branches—legislative, executive, and judicial—each is marked by distinctive state characteristics. The California legislature, for example, shares law-making authority with the people through the *initiative* process; the governor's power is diminished by the popular election of seven other executive officials; lower-court judges are chosen by the voters for six-year terms (although most of them begin their judicial careers as *gubernatorial* appointees).

Many of the freedoms guaranteed in the state constitution are identical to those protected by the U.S. Constitution. However, the state constitution includes additional rights for its residents. For example, Article I, Section 1, of the California constitution proclaims that "All people are by nature free and independent and have inalienable rights. Among these are enjoying and defending life and liberty, acquiring, possessing, and protecting property, and pursuing and obtaining safety, happiness, and privacy." Similar references to property acquisition, safety, happiness, and privacy are nowhere to be found in the U.S. Constitution.

California's constitution is much easier to amend than the federal Constitution, and it has been amended (and thus lengthened) over 500 times since 1879. The process involves two steps. First, amendments may be proposed either by a two-thirds vote in both houses of the legislature or by an *initiative* petition signed by 8 percent of the number of voters who voted in the last election for governor. Second, the proposed amendment must appear as a *proposition* on the ballot and must be approved by a simple majority of voters. As a result of the options created by the Progressives, voters can amend the state constitution without any legislative action.

Because the authors of initiative measures, as well as the voters, rarely distinguish between propositions which create laws and those which amend the constitution, the document has been burdened with many policies that should be *statutes* rather than parts of the permanent state charter. Over the years, the state constitution has become excessively long and detailed, and because so many aspects of state government seem to be inefficient or unresponsive to the public, there are periodic Constitutional Revision Commission reports that attempt to develop major changes to the document. However, these reports are rarely fully implemented. For the foreseeable future, it appears that California's constitution will remain as oversized and complex as its territory and population.

Questions to Consider

Using Your Text and Your Own Experiences

1. Who were the first Californians? Why were they so thoroughly destroyed by those who came next?

2. What is the most important contribution of the progressive movement in California?

3. What are some ways that California's history impacts life today, including culture, politics, ethnic diversity, immigration, and so on?

Notes

1. Sucheng Chan and Spencer Olin, *Major Problems in California History,* Houghton Mifflin, 1997, p. 30.
2. Cited by Alexander Cockburn, "Beat the Devil," *The Nation,* 24 June 1991, p. 839.
3. Antonia I. Castaneda, "Spanish Violence Against Amerindian Women," in Adela de la Torre and Beatriz Pasquera, eds., *Building with Our Hands: New Directions in Chicano Studies,* University of California Press, 1993.
4. "Conflicts over Land in a New State, 1850s–1870s," in Sucheng Chan and Spencer C. Olin, eds., *Major Problems in California History,* Houghton Mifflin, 1997, pp. 110–135.
5. Stephanie S. Pincetl, *Transforming California: A Political History of Land Use and Development,* Johns Hopkins University, 1999, p. 174.
6. W. J. Rorabaugh, "Berkeley in the 1960s," in Sucheng Chan and Spencer Olin, eds., *Major Problems in California History,* Houghton Mifflin, 1997, pp. 375–384.

CHAPTER 4

Freedom and Equality: California's Delicate Balance

"California is not so much poor as it is unequal."
Robert Enoch Buck, sociologist

People in California, as everywhere else in a capitalist democracy, must continually reassess choices regarding personal freedom and social equality. *Civil liberties*, such as freedoms of speech, press, and association (which restrict government powers), may conflict with *civil rights*, which often require government protections. For example, freedom of association can conflict with antidiscriminatory civil rights laws. Even though the state's Unruh Civil Rights Act was passed in 1959, some clubs and individuals are still claiming First Amendment freedom as reason to exclude women, unmarried couples, atheists, and homosexuals. Traditionally underrepresented ethnic groups and socioeconomically disadvantaged communities continue to battle unequal conditions. The courts are often the last resort to resolve civil rights and civil liberties. Equal rights advocates now include Inglewood High School students, who sued the State Department of Education on the grounds that inadequate college preparatory courses are offered in low-income communities, and ethnic organizations seeking legislation to end "racial profiling" or "DWB" (Driving While Black or Brown), in which police pull over motorists based on color.[1]

Freedom and Social Responsibility: Juggling Between Extremes

In numerous areas where individual freedom (or corporate profits) may conflict with public needs, California's policies have shifted gradually from endorsing maximum personal freedom to placing some limits on that freedom in order to maximize the well-being of the larger society and to protect the privacy of individuals. After many years of debate, the state legislature passed a law to create statewide antismoking standards while allowing cities to enact even stricter standards. Then the voters passed Prop. 10 (1998) to increase taxes on cigarettes and spend the funds on children's health care. Despite several well-funded attempts by the Tobacco Institute to overturn these laws, the public and politicians have held firm on the rights of nonsmokers. Similar public health measures include the increasing regulation of health maintenance organizations (HMOs), improved protections of senior citizens from "elder abuse," and stricter rules for teenaged drivers. Battles over individual privacy in the Internet age have become more urgent as the legislature debates legislation regarding access to insurance, banking, and medical records, as well as ways to protect Californians from cyber-stalking and identity fraud.[2] In the arena of environmental quality, the traditional struggle between public well-being and business bottom lines has evolved into more cooperative approaches. With the support of both environmentalists and major industries, the San Joaquin Valley Air Pollution Control District launched a $44 million plan to study the sources of smog in the Central Valley. Business interests such as the Western State Petroleum Association express hopes that those plans will avoid costly regulations which will hurt their profitability, but they acknowledge that something must be done to avoid federal penalties if air quality does not improve.[3] In a similar battle, the Los Angeles Regional Water Quality Control Board denied the business community's appeals about high costs and demanded that all new developments include plans to collect or filter rainwater so that polluted rainwaters do not end up in local beaches.[4]

In another arena, California courts have ruled that personal freedom includes the right *not* to hear a prayer at a public school graduation ceremony. In deference to the vast diversity of religious beliefs among Californians, the state Supreme Court determined that such prayers and invocations are an establishment of religion in violation of the separation of church and state. Despite this ruling, many public schools still offer prayers at football games, graduations, and other tax-sponsored events.

Equality: A Continuing Challenge

Along with their controversial struggles over personal freedom and societal responsibility, Californians have also been forced to confront a long history of racial bigotry. Prejudicial attitudes and discriminatory behaviors are older than the state itself. Only 10 percent of the Native Californians survived the Spanish era, and the first governor after statehood called for the extermination of those who remained. When the United States defeated Mexico in 1848, California Mexicans were gradually marginalized, losing much of the political and economic power they once wielded. Soon after, in the period of economic stagnation of the 1870s, the Chinese immigrants who helped build the transcontinental railroads during the 1860s became the targets of serious forms of racism, including lynchings and the "Chinese exclusion" provision of the 1879 state constitution (which attempted to prohibit Chinese from holding many kinds of jobs).

In today's multicultural California, the issues of equity are more complex than ever. With the passage of Prop. 209 (1996), the initiative to end affirmative action programs in all public agencies, the public polarized between those who believe that racial and ethnic discrimination still exists and must be remedied by conscious efforts and those who believe that "enough has been done for minorities already." Opponents of the proposition took their concerns to court and ultimately lost. Since further attempts to repeal Prop. 209 have not met with success, it appears that voters prefer that ethnicity not be considered in determining who gets the scarce resources of the state.

Meanwhile, racial tensions exist not only between whites and various minorities, but among minority groups themselves. In urban school districts, high schools may be homes to competing ethnic gangs whose rivalry erupts in periodic violence between some combination of Latinos, African-Americans, Asians, or Middle Eastern ethnic groups. Even inside the prison system, inmates of different ethnic groups are often segregated as a technique to avoid violence.

The conflicts among many of California's ethnic groups no doubt reflect the continuing difficulties that all people of color have in competing for scarce opportunities. (See Figure 4.1.) Although the law prohibits discrimination in employment, subtle limitations exist for nonwhite groups. In the rapidly expanding and highly competitive entertainment industry, opportunities for people of color continue to be rare. Despite the

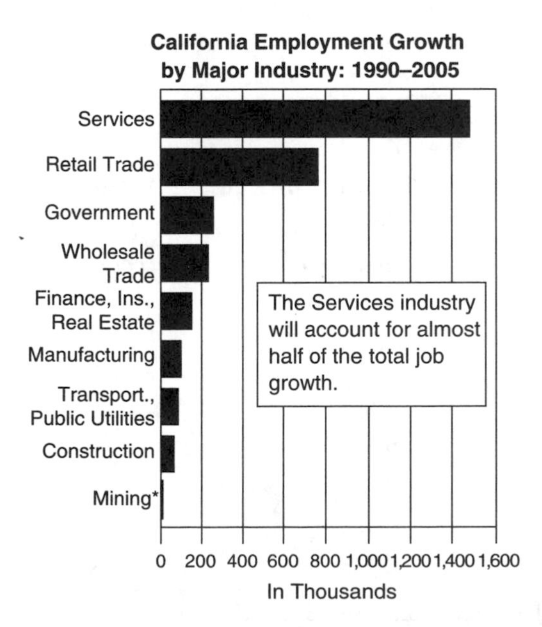

FIGURE 4.1 Targeting Training to Industry and Occupational Trends

*Mining employment is projected to decline by 2,000.

Source: Employment Development Department, Labor Market Division.

handful of well-known blacks and Latinos in the field, membership statistics for both the Writers Guild of America and the Screen Actors Guild indicate the work yet to be done on fully integrating these potentially lucrative fields. In a very different industry, as recently as spring 2000, a federal judge ordered shipping companies and the longshore union to pay nearly $3 million in damages to hundreds of minorities who failed a biased employment test used to determine who could become a dockworker.[5]

Similar forms of discrimination exist in access to vital technologies and high-tech training. While much of the problem is actually socioeconomic rather than ethnicity based, the fact remains that only 18 percent of Latino households and 27 percent of African-American households have computers in the home, while over 40 percent of white and Asian-American homes have computer access.[6] This lack of access prevents many Latino and African-American youth from being competitive in the labor market.

One factor in the "digital divide" is the lack of computer education in California's public schools. While schools in affluent communities may find resources to purchase equipment and pay teachers, low-income, minority communities are severely underserved in this regard. Although school segregation has been illegal for over fifty years, public school children in California often attend schools in which one ethnic group dominates or where ethnic groups "self-segregate" and rarely mingle. Large urban school systems often are nearly 90 percent nonwhite, with *white flight* sending families to suburbs or to private schools. Test scores, graduation rates, college admission data, and other indicators of educational success are almost always lower at public schools attended by minorities (typically from low-income families), and the state continues to struggle with how best to educate the millions of limited-English-speaking students. Table 4.1 shows the educational attainment of California's adults, and Figure 4.2 indicates the high levels of drop-outs among the state's ethnic populations. At the university level, the decision by the

TABLE 4.1

Educational Attainment of Persons 18 Years of Age and Older, California, 1990 Census

Educational Attainment Level	*Number*	*Percentage*
Total persons	22,020,542	100.0
Less than 9th grade	2,352,017	10.7
9th to 12th grade, no diploma	3,114,969	14.1
High school graduate (includes equivalency)	5,080,909	23.1
Some college, no degree	5,246,699	23.8
Associate degree	1,649,596	7.5
Bachelor's degree	3,052,702	13.9
Graduate or professional degree	1,523,650	6.9

Source: 1990 Census of Population and Housing, Summary Tape File 3A.

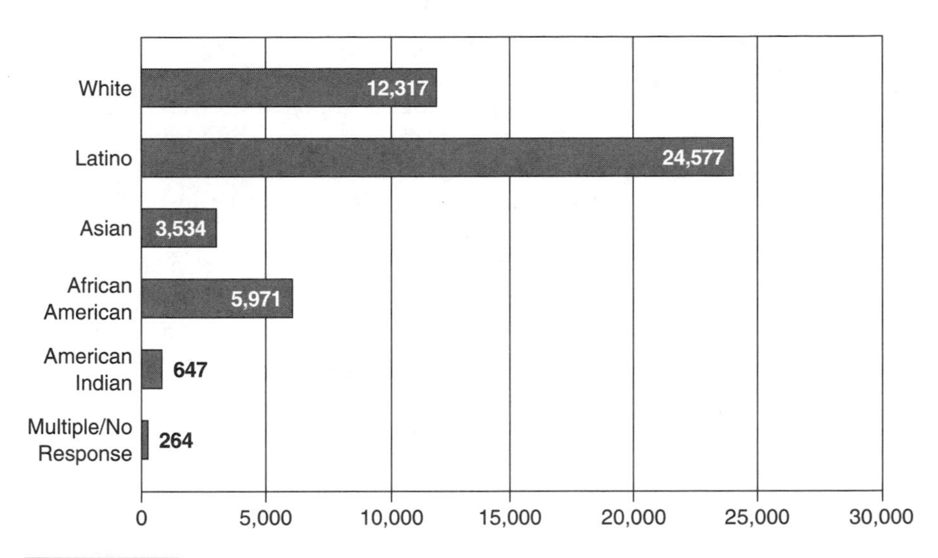

FIGURE 4.2 **Drop-outs from California Public Schools, 1997–1998**
Source: California Department of Education, Educational Demographics Unit—CBEDS.

Regents of the University of California to end affirmative action (before Prop. 209 passed) has already caused sharp reductions in the numbers of blacks and Latinos entering the UC system, particularly the prestigious law and medical schools.[7]

Diversity in Representation: Identity Politics in Action

In a continuing American tradition, when ethnic and immigrant communities grow larger, they begin to fight for their share of political and economic power. California's growing ethnic communities have already shifted the demographic pattern: there is no longer any one "majority" group. The state is populated by rapidly increasing populations of Latinos and Asians. By the year 2021, whites will make up about one-third of the population and thus will be a "minority" group, while Latinos, Asians and blacks together will comprise 60 percent (40 percent, 14 percent, and 6 percent, respectively).[8] However, this *demographic shift* does not automatically create an equally rapid shift in political power. Gains for underrepresented groups depend upon much more than their mere numbers. Factors which influence access to political power include their rates of voter registration and turnout, their financial ability to support candidates, and their interest in the political process. One structural change that appears to be helping more diverse candidates to win election is the voter-approved *term limits* law, which creates mandatory turnover in the state legislature and executive branch.

Although underrepresented groups may gradually benefit from term limits, their overall political effectiveness has been diminished by several factors. One is the lack of financial clout of many ethnic communities.

Because they are often excluded from well-paying jobs, they do not have the resources to support or recruit their own candidates. In addition, although blacks and native-born Latinos and Asians are citizens and eligible to vote, many of the new immigrants are not, thus losing out on the most fundamental political opportunity, the *franchise*. Despite the obstacles, changes have already begun in the distribution of political power among ethnic groups. The 1996 elections marked an important turning point for Latinos, as they voted in historically large numbers and helped elect a record-breaking number of legislators from their communities. Statewide, including every level of government, there are over 800 Latinos in elected office.[9] Cruz Bustamante, California's highest-ranking Latino politician, is the first Latino lieutenant governor.

As Latinos increase numerically, they have begun to live in many neighborhoods traditionally represented by African-American politicians. Over time it appears that African-Americans will decline numerically in proportion to the much faster-growing Latino and Asian groups, and African-American leaders are concerned about maintaining adequate representation. Some black politicians have made it a point to learn Spanish, as a way to bridge the gap with their Latino constituents.

Asian-Americans, in part because they do not tend to live in concentrated areas, are not electing members of their group in large numbers, yet are beginning to see gains at the local level. Like Latinos, whose numbers include people of eighteen different nationalities, Asian-Americans represent over thirty distinct national origins. Because the diversity is so enormous, there will never be precise and proportional representation for every ethnic group. Therefore, elected officials, regardless of their own background, must learn to represent everyone and not appeal to narrow ethnic concerns.

In addition to the largest ethnic and racial groups, small but active minority communities are working toward having a greater share of political power. Armenian-Californians have seen a governor from their heritage elected, while California's growing Islamic population has realized that not a single Muslim holds public office in California.[10] Native Americans in California, who compose over 120 tribal groups, have focused their political attention on issues relating to economic development on tribal land (with a heavy emphasis on building gambling casinos) and protection of their culture. With the state's social diversity likely to continue, political leadership in the twenty-first century will be a rainbow of cultures, all of which might retain their unique identities while also working to represent all Californians.

Sexual Politics: Slow Change for the Underrepresented

Women have made slow progress since the Women's Liberation movement of the 1960s raised concerns about women's equality and access to power. While women are 51 percent of the population, they are nowhere near having half of legislative seats, executive positions, judgeships, or local posts. Nonetheless, there are more women in office than anytime in California history, with ten (out of forty) in the Senate and twenty-four (out of eighty) in the Assembly. The state Supreme Court now has three (out of seven) women. Meanwhile, at the nonelected level, thousands of women who are state employees in agencies ranging from the Department of Motor Vehicles to the Employment Development Department earn only about three-fourths as much as men doing the same jobs.[11]

In a symbolic moment, the state's congressional delegation broke national records when Californians elected two women Senators, Barbara Boxer and Dianne Feinstein. They are joined in Washington, D.C., by sixteen women (out of California's fifty-two) in the House of Representatives. Since there are currently no *term limits* for federal officials, the women in Congress may remain in office for many years.

One often invisible and certainly underrepresented minority group is the gay and lesbian community. At one time, openly gay politicians were rare outside of San Francisco or West Hollywood, both magnets for the homosexual population. Now the state legislature has three "open" lesbian members, and numerous local governments have gay and lesbian elected officials. As more gays come *"out of the closet"* and become politically active, their clout will no doubt increase. However, the gay community has *partisan* differences, with gay Republicans fighting hard for respect in their party and gay Democrats highlighting the openness of their party's policies.

California's record of electing politicians with diverse backgrounds is certainly better than that of many other states. But perhaps it is inevitable that California take the lead, since the demographic pattern of increasing diversity is unlikely to change, and trends suggest that the nation will gradually come to look more like California in the twenty-first century.

Questions to Consider

Using Your Text and Your Own Experiences

1. Discuss some the areas where individual freedom (or free enterprise) may conflict with social needs. What is your position on these issues?
2. In what arenas are ethnic "minorities" underrepresented? Why do these patterns persist even though California has no "majority" group?
3. What can be done to balance the needs of diverse ethnic groups with the needs of California as a whole?

Notes

1. Heather Carrigan, "Inglewood Students Sue for Equal Education," *Open Forum*, American Civil Liberties Union of Southern California, Fall 1999, Vol. 73, No. 4, p. 1.
2. California Laws 1999, *Los Angeles Times*, 1 January 1999, p. A3.

3. Eric Bailey, "Central Valley Looking for Ways to Fight Air Pollution," *Los Angeles Times,* 6 June 2000, p. A3.
4. Joe Mozingo, "Officials Seek to Ease Fears on Plan to Curb Storm Runoff," *Los Angeles Times,* 9 June 2000, p. B3.
5. Dan Weikel, $2.75 Million Ordered Paid to Minorities in Dockworker Case," *Los Angeles Times,* 10 June 2000, p. B1.
6. Elias Lopez et al., "A Coordinated Approach to Raising the Socio-Economic Status of Latinos in California," California State Library, California Research Bureau, March 2000, p. 27.
7. Kenneth R. Weiss, "Plans Seek More UC Pupils from Poorer Schools," *Los Angeles Times,* 12 May 1997, p. A1.
8. Armando Acuna, "Changes in State's Ethnic Balance Are Accelerating," *Los Angeles Times,* 20 October 1999, p. A3.
9. Mark Z. Barabak, "A New Breed of Latino Lawmaker," *Los Angeles Times,* 16 July 1997, p. A1.
10. Author interview with Salam al-Marayati, 21 May 1997, Glendale.
11. "State's Female Workers Paid Less than Men, Study Finds," *Los Angeles Times,* 25 April 1996, p. A21.

CHAPTER 5

Media Influences and Pressure Groups

"The power of the [media] determines what people will talk about and think about."

Theodore White, historian

In a democratic system, the attitudes of the public should be a primary basis for political decision making. These political attitudes are demonstrated in election results and develop from opinions formed by the influence of families, friends, religious institutions, schools, life experiences, the mass media, and pressure groups. In recent years, as Americans read less, television and radio talk shows and "chat rooms" on the Internet help shape public opinion in the way that newspapers once did. In a large and diverse state such as California, organized interest groups and the enormous number of media outlets are vital components of the political process.

The Mass Media: A Massive Influence

Although state government profoundly affects peoples' daily lives, most media tend to neglect state and local news in favor of more dramatic national and international events. Because political decision making is rarely exciting to observe, California's television and radio stations usually provide little reporting from Sacramento or the various county or city halls around the state. The only ongoing TV coverage of state politics is the legislature's own television program, which shows legislative proceedings on many cable stations throughout California. The larger newspapers cover state politics, while many local issues are reported primarily in smaller papers. For those with computer skills and access, information on state legislation as well as many city and county governments is available over the Internet. (See Appendix C for useful websites.)

Because of California's size, creating an image that is memorable and appealing to voters requires those running for statewide office to use the mass media extensively. Due to general social trends which have minimized newspaper reading and encouraged the public's heavy reliance on television and radio, candidates spend most of their funds for ads in the broadcast media even as they attempt to get editorial endorsements from newspapers. With the growth of the Internet, many candidates spread their message through websites and email, a relatively inexpensive way to reach people.

Image making is an expensive and essential business in California. The 1998 state election cost over $500 million for all candidates,[1] and no candidate for any office is considered "serious" by media or voters unless he or she has sufficient financial resources to run. Campaign funds are spent on various forms of communication, including television, radio, mailings, telephone calls, email, and person-to-person precinct walks, all of which are coordinated by high-cost campaign consultants. The larger the electoral district, the less likely that a campaign will include any personal contact but rather will depend upon mail and media. Critics charge that political information conveyed by the media emphasizes personality factors, attacks, and scandals rather than significant policy issues, but despite "peace pledges" and other gimmicks, most candidates eventually use negative campaigning to attract voter attention.

Economic Interest Groups: Pressure Where It Counts

Organized *pressure groups (lobbies)* are also important in shaping public opinion. These have been unusually influential in California politics and often aid individual candidates by providing them with publicity, financial contributions, and campaign workers. The most powerful groups are usually those with the most financial resources, including the majority of business interests and some of the larger unions, such as public school teachers and state prison guards. When a group supports a successful candidate, it then gains better access to that politician than most other individuals ever have.

Special-interest groups generally avoid direct affiliation with any political party, preferring instead to work with whichever politician is in office. Business groups usually prefer to help elect Republicans, while labor groups prefer Democrats. The influence of various interest groups is indicated, in part, by their wealth and the number of people who belong to or are employed by their organizations. Nearly all of California's most profitable corporations, including oil companies, insurance giants, utilities, banks, and telecommunications companies, are linked together in pressure groups such as the California Manufacturers and Technology Association, the Western States Petroleum Association, and the Pacific Telesis group.[2] Other major *private-sector* players in the lobbying game are the California Association of Realtors, the California Medical Association, the Trial Lawyers Association, and the Agricultural Producers. The California Teachers Association, the California Correctional Peace Officers Association, the California State Employees Association, the California Labor Federation, and many other groups represent labor interests, not necessarily in a unified manner. (See Table 5.1.)

TABLE 5.1

Lobbying Expenses
January 1995–December 1996, by Industry

Industry	*Total*	*Top Spender in Category*	*Amount*
Agriculture	$6,153,211	California Farm Bureau	$1,156,404
Education	$16,117,939	California Teachers Association	1,985,108
Entertainment/ recreation	$6,727,759	Circus Circus	1,067,859
Banking/ insurance	$28,965,837	State Farm Insurance	1,859,395
Government	$36,947,670	San Diego County	1,479,159
Health	$30,831,649	California Care Health Plans	$849,836
Labor unions	$8,736,787	California School Employees Association	1,599,545
Legal	$5,714,396	California Applicants' Attorneys	838,381
Lodging/ restaurants	$938,092	California Restaurants Association	344,224
Manufacturing/ industrial	$28,459,113	California Manufacturers Association	1,707,477
Merchandise/ retail	$3,173,226	Robinson's-May	468,014
Miscellaneous	$28,569,220	California Chamber of Commerce	2,100,380
Oil and gas	$15,220,828	Western States Petroleum Association	3,883,845
Political organizations	$728,496	California Federation of Republican Women	144,928
Professional/trade	$18,722,322	California Motor Car Dealers Association	1,063,187
Public employees	$4,038,691	Peace Officers Research Association	639,910
Real estate	$6,087,409	Irvine Company	745,572
Transportation	$5,170,784	Atchison, Topeka, & Santa Fe Railroad	263,083
Utilities*	$15,636,128	California Cogeneration Council	926,290
Total: All Lobbies	**$266,939,559**		

*Total expenditures by utilities include, in many cases, payments made in connection with administrative testimony before the California Public Utilities Commission.

Source: California Secretary of State, available from http://www.ss.ca.gov/prd/lexp/table1.htm

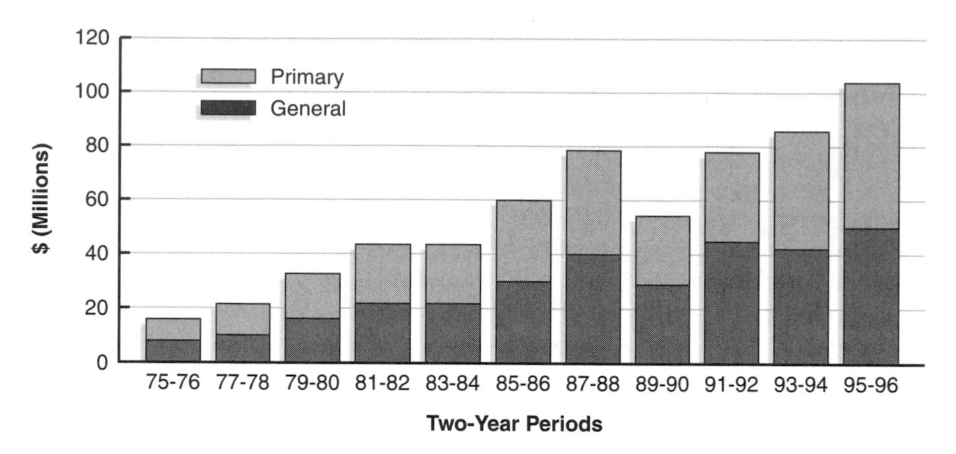

FIGURE 5.1 History of Campaign Costs: 1975–1996 Primary and General Election Candidates for State Legislature

Source: California Department of Finance.

Repeated attempts to curb the spending and influence of special interests have had limited success. Under the "free speech" rights guaranteed by the U.S. Constitution, courts have repeatedly ruled that limits on campaign contributions are a limit on free speech. This enables large organizations as well as affluent individuals to continue dominating campaign fundraising. The most recent effort to contain campaign contributions was Prop. 34 (November 2000), which was written by politicians and has been criticized for leaving too many "loopholes" for wealthy special interests. (See Figure 5.1.)

Other Interest Groups: Less Money, But Still a Voice

In addition to the business, professional, and labor groups which spend money to elect candidates through their *political action committees* (PACs) and later make contact with elected officials to share their views, California's political process has enabled less affluent interest groups to develop and participate. Such groups, discussed in the next chapter, include those representing various ethnic communities, environmental organizations such as the Planning and Conservation League, Children Now (which concerns itself with the needs of youth), and single-issue groups such as the California Abortion Rights Action League, Handgun Control, the Fund for Animals, and Surfriders (whose primary interest is in protecting beaches). These groups may not provide much campaign funding but may offer volunteers whose election support activities gain credibility for the organization.

In addition to an enormous array of nongovernmental lobbies, government agencies also lobby for their concerns, with numerous cities, counties, and *special districts*, such as water agencies and school districts, employing paid lobbyists in Sacramento. These government entities often seek funding or other legislative support from the state capitol.

Lobbyists in Action: A High-Skill, High-Pay Career

The term *lobbying* arose when those who wanted to influence elected officials would congregate in the lobbies of public buildings and wait to speak with a politician about their concerns. California's lobbyists, like those around the nation, gradually developed a pattern of wining and dining the politicians as well as giving them gifts and campaign contributions. Periodic scandals in which lobbyists and legislators were convicted of crimes involving trading money for votes created public demand for reform of the lobbying industry. The *1974 Political Reform Initiative* requires each lobbyist to file monthly reports showing income, expenditures, and steps taken to influence government action. This initiative also created the *Fair Political Practices Commission* (FPPC), which oversees campaigns and lobbying, and monitors any possible wrongdoing by candidates or PACs. The computer-literate person now has more opportunity to track political finances as a result of the Online Disclosure Act (1997), which requires all lobbying expenditures to be posted online at http://cal-access.ss.ca.gov (a site located within the Secretary of State's website).

The most recent voter-approved measure to control campaign spending was Prop. 34 (November 2000). This ballot measure was written and passed by the legislature and then approved by voters. Many political experts question whether the provisions are strict enough. Meanwhile, between 1986 and 1990, average contributions to Assembly and Senate campaigns increased by one-third.[3] Proposition 34 does not control spending by "independent expenditure campaigns," in which special-interest groups run ads and send mailers without coordinating their effort with the candidate.

In addition to helping favorable politicians get elected, lobbyists perform an assortment of tasks to achieve their organization's goals. Many lobbyists are former lawmakers or legislative aides, whose personal contacts enable them to work successfully in the halls of power. They earn substantial salaries for handling the following:

1. Campaign efforts to elect sympathetic candidates, especially incumbents
2. Testimony for or against bills being considered by legislative committees
3. Informal contacts with lawmakers for purposes of providing them with information, statistical data, and expert opinions on pending legislation
4. Ads and announcements in newspapers, on websites, and through direct mail which appeal to the public to take a position and convey their views to elected officials

5. Sponsorship of initiative or referendum petitions to put propositions on the ballot for the approval of the voters
6. Encouragement of pressure-group members to write letters to lawmakers regarding particular bills
7. Organization of protest marches and other forms of public demonstrations
8. Favorable publicity and endorsements for cooperative lawmakers inserted in the internal publications of the organization
9. Attempts to influence the appointment (by the governor) of sympathetic judges and administrative officials

With the passage of *term limits* (Prop. 140) in 1990, the influence of lobbyists has changed. Before term limits, lobbyists could develop ongoing friendships with legislators, who often spent decades in office. Now, legislators rotate out of office frequently, and lobbyists must quickly develop relationships with newly elected officials and their new staff members. However, those newly elected officials may be more susceptible to lobbyists, because lobbyists have much more experience in Sacramento than most new legislators.

Because lobbying still determines the outcome of almost all legislation, Californians who realize how much political decisions can affect their daily lives usually become interested in tracking the impact of lobbying on their elected officials. This involves checking campaign donation records plus legislators' voting records in order to find out how a particular group has influenced a specific legislator. A major source of information is the Secretary of State's Cal-Access website. For those interested in more direct involvement, the best solution may be to join those interest groups which reflect the individual's values and political concerns. Many lobbies are open groups which welcome new members, including organizations involved with environmental issues, ethnic concerns, health care, and many more (see Appendix A). Members receive updates from lobbyists indicating what legislation is being considered and how the individual can phone or write in a timely, informed manner (see Appendix D). While any individual Californian can always write a letter, the most effective political action comes through organized groups.

Questions to Consider

Using Your Text and Your Own Experiences

1. How many ways does mass media influence political attitudes? Give examples of those influences. Remember that media includes both the information media and the entertainment media.
2. What makes a special-interest group powerful? Are there problems with how much power some of these groups have?

3. Is personal wealth an essential ingredient for individual political influence? If you are not wealthy, what can you do to have a voice in California's political process?

Notes

1. Dan Morain, "Wealth Buys Access to State Politics," *Los Angeles Times,* 18 April 1999, p. A1.
2. "Top 10 Lobbyist Employers Ranked from High to Low," January 1, 1999–September 30, 1999, Secretary of State 3rd Quarter report, http://www.ss.ca.gov/prd/lobreport99 3qtr/chart3.htm
3. Raymond J. La Raja and Dorie Apollonio, "Term Limits Affect Legislators' Fund Raising Prowess," *Institute of Governmental Studies Public Affairs Report, University of California,* Vol. 40, No. 5, September 1999, p. 3.

CHAPTER 6

Political Parties and Other Voluntary Associations

"The success of the Republican and Democratic parties is gauged by how they do at election time; electing their candidates is their primary focus."

Ken deBow and John Syer, political scientists

The two major parties seem to be of even less importance to the average Californian than to most Americans. Nearly 14 percent of California voters belong to no party ("decline to state" registration status), and another 6 percent are members of the minor parties, with these numbers increasing each year.[1] Many citizen activists remain almost entirely separate from party organizations yet are immersed in the grassroots political process through an enormous variety of voluntary associations, some of which, like many Parent Teacher Associations (PTAs) and homeowner groups, have become highly politicized. Activities which used to require volunteers with time and energy and little political awareness now require participants who understand the intimate links between one's neighborhood problems or local school issues and the larger California political process. Parents of children in dilapidated schools, homeowners concerned about graffiti, and beach lovers whose shores are polluted are among many Californians whose political involvement begins when they collect signatures for ballot initiatives or lobby public officials in an effort to resolve their particular problems.

Meanwhile, despite the small numbers of Californians who participate directly in their political parties or feel any special enthusiasm for either party, *party affiliations* are reflected in the voting patterns of legislators and the track records of governors. On many issues of major public concern, such as abortion, criminal justice, and funding for education, the majority party in the legislature can heavily influence the final outcome, and the votes of individual legislators may depend more on party allegiance than on any other factor.

Do Parties Matter? The Voters' Perspective

California's tradition of minimal loyalty to either of the two major parties has roots in the state constitution's rules regarding state employment and elections. California's *civil service system* fills 98 percent of all state government jobs on the basis of competitive exams, thereby reducing the number of jobs that can be used as *patronage* to reward supporters of the winning party. Local offices (including city, county, and education boards) and all judicial elections are *nonpartisan*, with candidates listed by name and occupation, with no mention of party affiliation. The ballot format itself, known as the *office-block* ballot, groups candidates under the heading of the office being contested rather than in columns divided according to party, and thus encourages voters to concentrate on individual candidates rather than voting a straight party ticket. The nonpartisan nature of most California politics is best understood in terms of the fact that only 179 of the 19,279 elective offices throughout the state are *partisan*.[2]

Although the parties are not as well organized nor as meaningful to voters as they are in some other states, Californians display some partisan loyalty. Many voters registered in a party still vote for their party's candidates without much thought, and the enormous amounts of campaign funds spent on media are often aimed at the 20 percent of voters who are not registered with either major party and therefore are considered "up for grabs" or *swing votes*. Table 6.1 shows that many voters are not affiliated with the major parties.

Differences between Democrats and Republicans show up very clearly on matters such as taxation, aid to low-income Californians, and other major fiscal battlegrounds in the legislative arena. Almost all Republicans continue to favor tax cuts for business and the upper middle class, while Democrats are somewhat more willing to maintain tax rates to support public education and other programs. Even as the two parties have their differences, the differences within them are perhaps equally important. Moderate Republicans are under severe pressure from the "Christian

TABLE 6.1

Voter Registration Patterns, 1950–2000, Showing Decreased Affiliation with Major Parties

	Democrat	*Republican*	*Other Party*	*Decline to State*
1950	58%	35%	1%	4%
1960	57%	38%	1%	3%
1970	55%	39%	2%	4%
1980	53%	34%	3%	9%
1990	49%	39%	3%	9%
2000	46%	35%	5%	14%

Source: California Secretary of State.

right" to adopt its anti-abortion, anti-gay rights policies, while mainstream Democrats are reminded by their more liberal colleagues about supporting gay rights, gun control, and environmental protection.

With all the internal and interparty dissension, it is perhaps no wonder that many citizens register their disaffection by refusing to vote at all or by registering to vote without affiliating with either major party. In the June 1998 gubernatorial primary, only 70 percent of eligible citizens were registered to vote.[3]

Minor Parties: Alternative Political Voices

Although the state constitution makes it exceedingly difficult for minor parties to get on the ballot, California voters manage to show their frustration with the two major parties in diverse ways. Between 1966 and 1998, the percentage of voters registered as either Democrats or Republicans dropped from 94 percent to 81 percent.[4] Among the other party options are the Libertarian (advocates of *minimalist* government), American Independent (extremely conservative), Natural Law (belief in meditation as a political solution), Reform (Ross Perot's party), and the Greens (environmental focus). These parties remain official parties with *ballot status* as long as they receive 2 percent of the vote for any statewide office.

Then there is the small minority of Californians who belong to the category "Other" and have identified themselves as members of parties known as "Halloween," "Let's Have a," "Utopian Immoralist," "Smash the State," "Marijuana," and numerous other inventive titles.[5] Despite the seeming frivolity of these fanciful (or imaginary) parties, the official minor parties occasionally pull enough votes away from a major-party candidate to cause an electoral surprise or *upset*.

Party Organization: Who Makes the Rules?

California's parties are regulated both by state law and by their own internal guidelines. The general structure of the two major parties is identical, with each having a state central committee and fifty-eight *county committees*. The most powerful nonelected official in each party is the state party chair, although this individual is rarely well known by the general public. Beyond these two committees, much of party organization is left to each party. Democrats have organized themselves into Assembly district committees, while Republicans rely primarily on county committees for their local activities. (See Figure 6.1.) These activities include recruiting candidates, raising money, registering voters, and supporting party nominees in general elections.

This level of political activity involves only a small fraction of the population. Of the 20 million Californians eligible to vote, only 70 percent even bother to register, and, of those, only 8.6 million (41 percent

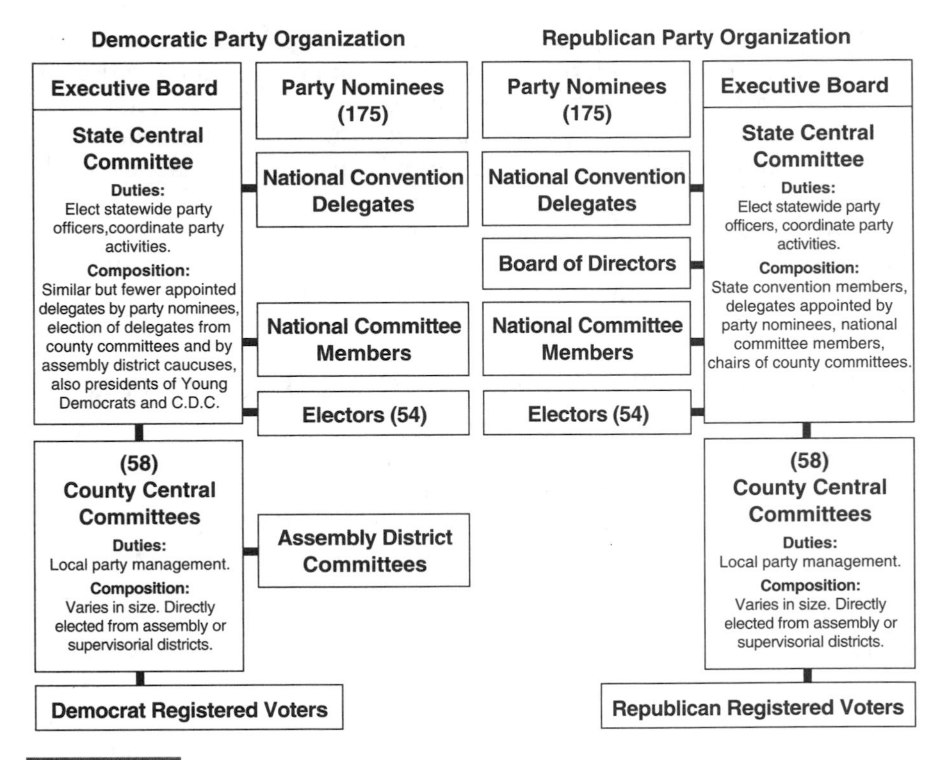

FIGURE 6.1 Political Party Organization
Source: California Government and Politics Annual.

of eligibles) actually voted in the 1998 gubernatorial election.[6] Turnout for the March 2000 presidential primary was the highest in twenty years, with credit going to the *blanket primary* created by Prop. 198 (1996), which allowed all voters to select candidates from a "blanket" list including every candidate from all seven official parties. However, soon after that primary, the U.S. Supreme Court agreed with a legal challenge sponsored by a united front of Democrats and Republicans by ruling that the blanket primary harms parties by allowing nonmembers to select party nominees. By the next state primary, it is probable that some form of *closed primary* will be used. This method of selecting party nominees allows only those registered in a party to vote on that party's candidates. Another possibility might allow "decline to state" voters to vote in any party's primary if the party permits it. This solution may actually encourage the growth of "decline to state" voters and reduce the power of parties.

Despite their victory in the courts regarding primary elections, California's parties are generally viewed as weak. In order to overcome the structural "antiparty" bias of the state constitution, the two major parties attempt to create stronger internal structures by promoting "clubs" or caucuses. The Republican Party's very conservative Young Americans for Freedom (YAF) claims to "hold the reigns of power" in the party,[7] while the liberal California Democratic Council is the Democratic Party's largest club. Other small groupings include the Log Cabin Club (Republican gay rights group) and the Democrats for Neighborhood Action (a Los Angeles-based group that has helped elect numerous officials). In general, these internal organizations have only an indirect impact on the larger political process.

Perhaps because parties are not very powerful, and because most party activists are unknown and unrecognized, many Californians choose to be active politically without being involved in parties.

Outside Parties: Nonpartisan Political Organizations

Outside the party structure and party-oriented organizations are the multitude of *grassroots* groupings which for many people are California politics. Perhaps the growing popularity of such groups reflects the historical weakness of parties and the current low profiles of the partisan organizations. Or perhaps the issues that confront Californians daily are best approached through *issue-oriented organizations* with no absolute loyalty to any party.

For those concerned with environmental protection, groups such as Save Our Coast (based in San Mateo), the Labor/Community Strategy Center (in Los Angeles), the League of Conservation Voters (statewide), and the Group Against Spraying People (Camarillo) are in constant need of volunteers' time, energy, and money. For women seeking greater representation, the California chapters of the National Women's Political Caucus, the California Abortion Rights Action League, and the Los Angeles-based Fund for a Feminist Majority all raise money and organize volunteers to get women into office as well as to elect men sympathetic to feminist concerns.

African-American and Latino activists are often involved in California affiliates of the Southern Christian Leadership Conference, the National Association for the Advancement of Colored People, the Southwest Voter Registration and Education Project, the Mexican American Political Association, and the Mexican American Legal Defense and Education Fund, all of which encourage minority involvement in both electoral politics and community issues. Asian-Americans, rivaling Latinos as the fastest-growing minority group, derive much of their political clout from the Asian Pacific American Legal Center and the Asian Pacific Policy Institute, both in Southern California. All of these groups concern themselves with the ongoing issues of minorities, including access to employment, education, and housing, as well as adequate representation in politics and media.

Other forms of voluntary associations which bring people together include the Bus Riders Union (supporting low-cost transportation), Californians for Pesticide Reform, local homeowner and resident associations, and numerous *ad hoc* committees that come together for short-term purposes, such as planting trees or preventing unwanted development projects. California's organized historic preservationists battle to protect architectural and cultural landmarks from demolition, while Neighborhood Watch committees, formed by small groups of neighbors in coordination with local police departments, carry out important tasks such as painting out graffiti, reporting abandoned cars, and keeping track of crime. Voluntary groups whose issues become the focus of widespread concern can ultimately create major changes, such as the "Three Strikes, You're Out" laws that exist in part due to the political organizing done by families damaged by violent crime.

Californians in search of the California dream have two clear options: they can "cocoon" into the privacy of their homes and try to block out the social stresses around them, or they can join other concerned people to work toward improvement in the quality of life. Literally hundreds of organizations exist through the volunteer efforts of people who want to make a difference. The only limits on political participation are the time and energy of people, who may find that their "voluntary" political participation soon begins to feel "essential." Once the connections between individual problems and the political process are made, it becomes difficult to return to a narrow, nonpolitical life.

Questions to Consider

Using Your Text and Your Own Experiences

1. What are some issues in everyday life that are impacted by political decision makers? Discuss the importance of understanding this connection between daily life and politics.

2. How important are political parties? Why is there an increase in people registering "decline to state" or in a minor party? What other type of organization can people join to express their political concerns?

3. Debate the closed vs. the blanket (or "open") primary. Which one is favored by the established political parties? Which do you favor? Why?

Notes

1. Tracy Thomas, "California Voters by Party," *Los Angeles Times,* 7 March 2000, P. A3.
2. David G. Savage, "Nonpartisan Vote Challenge Voided," *Los Angeles Times,* 18 June 1991, p. A3.
3. Mark Dicamillo, "Californians Vote in the State's First Blanket Primary," *Institute of Governmental Studies Public Affairs Report, University of California Berkeley,* Vol. 39, No. 5, September 1998, p. 1.
4. Edward J. Boyer, "Voters Push for Independence," *Los Angeles Times,* 3 March 2000, p. B2.
5. Ray Reynolds, *California the Curious,* Bear Flag Books, 1989, p. 168.
6. Mark Baldassare, *California in the New Millenium,* University of California Press, 2000, p. 11.
7. Bud Lembke, "Pulse Beats," in *Political Pulse,* quoting California Young Americans for Freedom newsletter, August 27, 1999, p. 6.

CHAPTER 7

Campaigns and Elections

"Money is the mother's milk of politics."
Former California Assembly Speaker Jess Unruh

Public officials are chosen in a two-step process involving both primary and runoff or general elections. California's primary process has undergone changes recently due to voter-approved measures followed by negative court decisions. The voters had a chance to use a form of "open" or *blanket primary* in 1998 (gubernatorial) and 2000 (presidential), but soon after, California was forced by federal court order to return to the *closed primary* system, in which voters may only choose from candidates in their own party. The blanket primary permitted all voters to select from a "laundry list" of all candidates—a system which empowers voters but reduces the power of political parties to control the selection of their candidates. This open system was credited with a better-than-usual voter turnout. In a closed primary, those registered "decline to state" (no party) do not select any party's candidates, but may vote for nonpartisan offices and ballot measures. Politicians, including Governor Davis, who support permitting "decline to state" voters to have a vote in nomination primaries are seeking ways to empower those who prefer not to join a party—a growing percentage of the electorate.

Primaries are traditionally held in spring, and any registered voter may run for an office in the primary by filing a declaration of candidacy with the county clerk at least sixty-nine days before the election, paying a filing fee (unless granted an exemption based on inability to pay), and submitting a petition with the signatures of from twenty to five hundred registered voters, depending on the office sought. In a partisan primary designed to select party candidates, the party nomination is won by the candidate with the *plurality* of votes. In a nonpartisan contest, such as for county supervisor, one candidate must get a true majority in order to win. Therefore, if no candidate in the nonpartisan primary receives a *majority* (50 percent plus one), the two with the most votes face one another in a later *runoff election*. Nonpartisan elections are held for city, county, judicial, and education offices. These elections (with the exception of county races) are usually held in odd-numbered years.

In general elections, held in early November of even-numbered years for state and national offices, the ballot includes the nominees from each party for each office and all propositions which have qualified for that ballot. Most voters still go to the *polls* to vote, but an increasing number take advantage of *absentee ballots* to vote at home and mail their ballots, thus saving the time it may take to vote in person. Anyone may request an absentee ballot, and in 2000 approximately one-fourth of voters voted in the privacy of their homes and mailed in their ballots.[1] In some places, such as Riverside and Monterey, voters are experimenting with paperless elections by using touch-screen computer voting in public libraries and shopping malls.[2]

California Politicians: See How They Run

It is relatively easy to run for office in California, but to win requires a combination of campaign ingredients that may be difficult to assemble. One of the most important is an "electable" candidate. Because of the many voters who are recent arrivals in the state and the frequency with which they move, a candidate's longstanding community ties and a wide personal acquaintance are not as important here as elsewhere in the nation. Name recognition is important, however, and candidates spend a good deal of time and money to try to imprint their names in the memories of voters.

Political dynasties are built when a familiar name becomes an electoral asset, such as the Los Angeles-based Hahn family (father Kenny was a county supervisor and son Jim is mayor and daughter Janice is on the city council) and the Browns (former Governor Pat was the father of Oakland Mayor Jerry and former state Treasurer Kathleen). Even mistaken identity can benefit a candidate when a coincidental "same last name" individual runs in an area where a popular politician's name still draws votes. Similarly, the widows of elected officials are often chosen to replace their husbands, in part due to name recognition. Both Mary Bono (R, Palm Springs) and Lois Capps (D, Santa Barbara) were elected to complete the congressional terms of their deceased husbands.

Money and Politics: The Vital Link

In part because name recognition is so important, and because it takes a lot of money to create that, California campaigns are now so expensive that one of the greatest dangers to democratic politics is that races are often won by the biggest spenders, not necessarily the best candidates. Until recently, *incumbents* typically had the advantage in terms of finances and name recognition, but both *term limits* and the recent trend toward extremely wealthy individuals spending millions to create name identification has altered the situation. Open races in which there is no incumbent sometimes result in a more level playing field for candidates; however, wealthy individuals such as Richard Riordan, former mayor of Los Angeles, can buy name recognition by spending enormous sums on media and mailers.

Both incumbents and *challengers* spend much of their campaign funds on media, especially radio and television ads. The increasing use of the Internet to promote campaigns is relatively inexpensive but still reaches only the techno-literate population, and most campaign strategists do not rely on the Web to mount a successful campaign. Although TV ads are not efficient because they reach so many nonvoters, they are still essential components of most statewide campaigns and, for local races, may utilize local cable channels to target voters. Every election season, politicians spend enough money on campaigns to cover the costs of some of the most needed services in the state. Each election sets new records for campaign spending, with the 1998 state election costing over $350 million.[3] Many police officers, teachers, firefighters, and mental health workers in the state would gladly have seen those same hundreds of millions spent on the services they strive to provide. Under Prop. 34's voluntary campaign spending limits, candidates may agree to limit their spending, but it is too soon to tell whether any candidate will actually do so.

In addition to media purchases, campaign costs include political consultants' fees, polling costs, and direct mail to voters. Direct mail has become an intricate business in which experts help candidates mail persuasive literature to *target audiences*. In tight races, where *swing voters* may make the difference, one brochure targets conservatives while another appeals to liberals. Another frequent strategy is to avoid mentioning party affiliation in order to appeal to the many Californians who are registered *decline to state*. Like other Americans, Californians turn out to vote in proportion to the amount of media attention and controversy generated by an election; conservative voters made sure to vote for Prop. 22 (March 2000) as a statement against gay marriage, while liberals were urged to turn out to vote "no" on school vouchers, which would allow public dollars to be spent on private schools (November 2000).

The millions of campaign dollars come from a variety of sources. The Fair Political Practices Commission, set up by voters in 1974 through the initiative process, keeps records of donations. The pattern of donations continues to show high spending by special-interest groups, which now also benefit from their own independent-expenditure campaigns, in which they promote candidates or ballot measures separately from the official campaigns. Top campaign spenders include virtually the same list of pressure groups that also lobby Sacramento throughout the year: oil companies, utilities, telecommunications businesses, banks, agribusinesses, insurance corporations, doctors, lawyers, labor unions, teachers, and prison guards.

While most campaigning is done with dollars, California voters occasionally get a taste of the more personal campaign styles of the past. During election season, those who are registered to vote may answer the doorbell and find a campaign staff member or volunteer coming to chat. Occasionally, the candidate actually visits in person; however, only a candidate who is very dedicated or reasonably well-to-do can afford to quit work to campaign on a daily basis. Door-to-door personal efforts are most effective in local races, where even a less well funded newcomer can defeat an incumbent when the electorate's mood is right.

Elections Without Candidates: Direct Democracy

Our federal system is a *representative democracy* in which voters elect officials to make decisions for them. The federal system has no form of direct citizen decision making: every decision is made by elected officials. However, states may choose to develop their own forms of *direct democracy*, in which voters may bypass elected officials to make laws themselves or even to remove elected officials from office. California's direct democracy was created by the Progressives of the early 1900s as part of their strategy to bring political power back to the people, and Californians have made ample use of this opportunity. California's constitution assures that the state's voters can make laws, amend the state constitution, repeal laws, or recall their elected officials through the ballot box.

The most commonly used of the three forms of direct democracy is the *initiative*. The *initiative* permits registered voters to place a proposed law, or *statute*, on the ballot through petition signatures equal to 5 percent of the votes cast in the last election for governor. Similarly, voters may propose amendments to the state constitution (which requires 8 percent of voters to achieve ballot status). Petition circulators are given 150 days in which to gather signatures. At that time, the Secretary of State receives the petitions and evaluates whether enough valid signatures have been collected. If there are enough signatures, the measure is given a proposition number and can be approved by a simple majority in the next election. Due to the high costs of qualifying an initiative and promoting its passage, the large majority of initiatives on the ballot are written and promoted by organized special-interest groups, which usually pay professional signature gatherers to qualify propositions to appear on the ballot.

Less frequently used are *referendums*, of which there are two types. One type allows voters to repeal a law passed by the legislature. Due to the requirement that all signatures must be gathered within a mere ninety days of the legislation's passage, this type of referendum has rarely appeared on the ballot. The second type of referendum is one submitted to the voters by the legislature rather than by petition; this is most frequently used for state bonds.

The third component of direct democracy is the *recall*. It is a device by which voters can petition for a special election to remove an official from office before his or her term has expired. The threat of recall is more common than its actual usage, and the threat can sometimes cause a politician to change positions on an issue or even to resign. A recall petition normally requires the signatures of 12–25 percent of those who voted in the last election; if that requirement is met, opposing candidates may file for places on the ballot. Voters must then vote on whether or not to recall the official and which of the other candidates to elect to fill the possible vacancy. Unlike impeachment, which is initiated by the legislature itself, the recall begins with the voters (or a special-interest group that taps voter outrage).

Direct Democracy: Pros and Cons

The Progressives intended for the initiative, referendum, and recall to be methods by which citizens could make policy directly or remove incompetent officials, thus counteracting the corruption of state or local officials who might be too subservient to powerful special interests. Instead, those same special interests have grown sophisticated in their use of these mechanisms to achieve their goals. Since the signatures of about 420,000 registered voters are necessary to place a statutory initiative on the ballot (and over 670,000 are required for a constitutional amendment), and because signature gatherers must get twice as many as required in order to offset the many invalid signatures found by the Secretary of State, it can easily require nearly $1 million just to qualify a measure. Costs to publicize the measure (by those favoring and those opposing it) can go into the multimillion-dollar range—just for one controversial proposition. Another problem is that there are no limits on the number of propositions per election—voters may become overwhelmed by the work required to read and evaluate dozens of ballot measures. Yet another problem with initiatives is that measures may pass by large margins yet still have unconstitutional elements which the courts then negate. As to the recall, critics suggest that it can be used unfairly against a competent but unpopular official.

Most political experts and politicians believe that California's direct democracy needs reform. Ideas for improvement include the possibility of having a legal review of propositions before they are circulated for signatures, changing the time limits for signature gathering, making it easier for the legislature to amend initiatives without returning to the voters, and enforcing the requirement that initiatives deal with only one subject.

Perhaps one reason that it is so difficult to reform the direct democracy process is that it still serves one function: to remove power from elected officials and grant that power to the voters. In some sense direct democracy adds a fourth element to the checks and balances of the three branches of government, one in which the voters themselves find a voice—a voice which may differ enormously from the ones emanating from the halls of government in California.

TABLE 7.1

Ballot Measures At a Glance, November 7, 2000

Proposition		*Description*
32	Y	Veteran's Bond Act of 2000
33	N	Legislature. Participation in Public Employee's Retirement System. Legislative Constitutional Amendment
34	Y	Campaign Contributions and Spending. Limits. Disclosure. Legislative Initiative Amendment.
35	Y	Public Works Projects. Use of Private Contractors for Engineering and Architectural Services. Initiative Constitutional Amendment and Statute.
36	Y	Drugs. Probation and Treatment Program. Initiative Statute.
37	N	Fees. Vote Requirements. Taxes. Initiative Constitutional Amendment.
38	N	School Vouchers. State-Funded Private and Religious Education. Public School Funding. Initiative Constitutional Amendment.
39	Y	School Facilities. 55% Local Vote. Bonds, Taxes. Accountability Requirements. Initiative Constitutional Amendment and Statute.

Y=passed N=not passed

Cleaning up Politics: Campaign Reform

Every few years it seems that there is yet another "campaign reform" initiative on the California ballot. Often, there are two conflicting initiatives dealing with the same issue. Over time, voters have approved restrictions on transfers of funds between candidates, required reporting of donations to the *Fair Political Practices Commission* (created by the 1974 Political Reform Act), and imposed strict limits on the amount a lobbyist can spend to "wine and dine" an elected official. Yet it seems that each time voters say "yes" to a reform, the unintended consequences of the law appear in later years and demonstrate the difficulty of separating money from politics. In California, thus far, no law has yet made it possible to run campaigns without large sums of money, and it remains to be seen whether the latest "campaign finance reform," Prop. 34 (November 2000), will restore any sense of fairness.

The Changing Electorate: Who Votes and Who Doesn't

With about one-quarter of the population being immigrants from other nations,[4] California's pool of eligible voters is proportionately smaller than that in most other states. However, recent political pressures have created a sense of urgency among immigrants to become citizens and voters. Traditionally, voter turnout in California is similar to that in other states: many fewer people vote than are eligible. It remains to be seen whether the new citizens will be dedicated voters and increase the general rate of participation. Nonvoters include the "contented apathetics," who just aren't interested in politics because they see no need to be; people who are devoting all their time to economic survival and don't have time or energy to become informed citizens; and those who are "politically alienated" and believe their vote makes no difference.[5] Voters tend to be affluent, educated, and older than average, leaving many younger, poorer, and less educated Californians underrepresented in the electoral process. Until ethnic minorities and lower-income citizens vote in larger numbers, the trend toward a multicultural state with a *monocultural* electorate will continue. Perhaps the ray of hope for the growing ethnic communities is that new citizens appear to be taking their franchise seriously, with Latino turnout improving noticeably since the 1996 elections.[6]

Having a real democracy requires time and energy from ordinary citizens. Otherwise, the few who bother to vote will exercise disproportionate power, and those they elect may feel responsible to fewer people, rather than to society as a whole.

Questions to Consider

Using Your Text and Your Own Experiences

1. Discuss the relationship between money and politics. What forms of power are available to average citizens who do not have large sums to give to candidates or PACs?
2. Debate the pros and cons of our direct democracy choices. Would California be better off without them or with a modified version?
3. Take a class survey. Pair up voters with nonvoters to discuss the issue of voter participation. Does your classroom reflect the *monocultural* electorate or a changing electorate? Can voters persuade nonvoters to use their franchise?

Notes

1. Miguel Bustillo, "Rise in Use of Absentee Ballots Alters Tactics as Election Day Nears," *Los Angeles Times,* 3 November 2000, p. A3.
2. Bud Lembke and Larry Lynch, "Touch-Screen Voting Trials Prove Popular, Could Lead to Much More Absentee Voting," *Political Pulse,* Vol. 15, No. 18, 19 November 1999, p. 1.
3. Dan Morain, "Governor Race Set Spending Record," *Los Angeles* Times, 2 April 1999, p. A1.
4. U.S. Census Bureau.
5. Richard Zeiger, quoting Mervin Field, "Few Citizens Make Decisions for Everyone," *California Journal,* November 1990, p. 519.
6. Ted Rohrlich, "Record Percentage of Latinos Turn out to Vote, Exit Poll Finds," *Los Angeles Times,* 9 April 1997, p. A1.

CHAPTER 8

The California Legislature

"I came up here to be a legislator, which I thought was like being an intellectual in action. What I found was I was an assembly worker in a bill factory."
Former Senator Tom Hayden (D, Santa Monica)

The California legislative branch is a bicameral body consisting of a forty-member Senate elected for a four-year term and an eighty-member Assembly elected for two. Half of the Senate and the entire Assembly are elected in November of even-numbered years.

Each Senate district must be equal in population to all other Senate districts, with the same rule holding for all Assembly districts. Thus, each Senate district includes twice as many residents as each Assembly district, and state Senators are considered to be more powerful than Assembly members. Each Senate district includes two Assembly districts. (See Figure 8.1.)

The State of the Legislature: Chaos in Motion?

Like many political bodies in the United States, California's legislature is the subject of concern and even mistrust among the public. Periodic scandals in which legislators are found guilty of political corruption get far more media coverage than the dull but essential work done by most others.[1] Battles between the Republican and Democratic *caucuses* or between the legislature and governor also get publicity if the matter is viewed as worthy of media attention, and this bickering and backbiting among public officials no doubt adds to the public's disdain for politics. Meanwhile, California's legislators have one of the nation's best pay and benefit packages, including steady raises (salaries are $99,000 per year) plus generous expense accounts. The independent citizens' commission which approved a 37% raise during the recession stated that higher salaries were needed to "attract qualified candidates."[2] Perhaps it is no wonder that

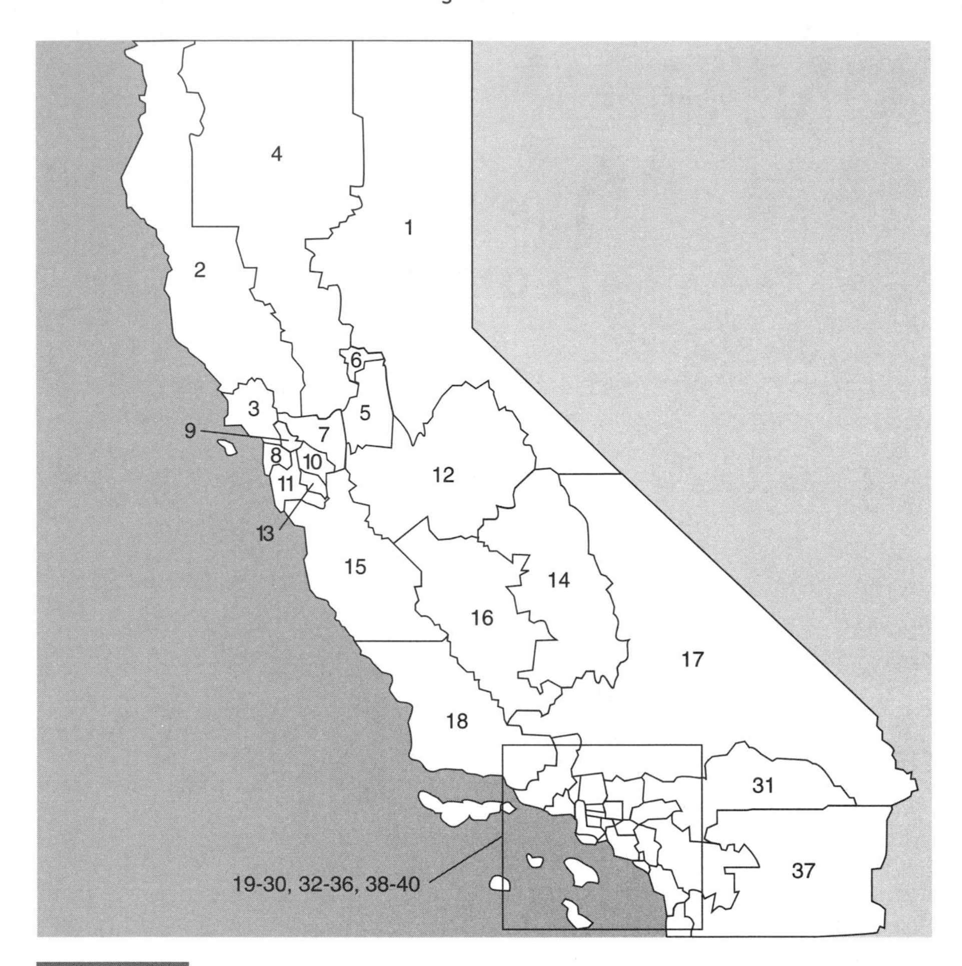

FIGURE 8.1 Senate Districts

Source: Senate Committee on Elections and Reappointment.

furious voters approved Prop. 140 (1990), which demanded strict *term limits* for legislators and executive-branch officials and also eliminated the legislators' pension plan.[3]

However, voters may not have realized the full impact of their term-limit decision. Along with the six-year limit on Assembly service and the eight-year limit on Senators, the proposition cut legislative budgets in ways which led to the loss of many highly skilled legislative staff members. In addition to the loss of experience of these personnel, term limits also leads to rapid turnover among legislators, which simply means more "rookies" creating our state's laws and more special-interest lobbyists using their unlimited years of experience to influence the novice legislators. A few long-time legislators, desperate to remain in office, have taken to moving to new districts so they can run again after reaching their term limit (the limits apply to a particular legislative district). Despite all these shortcomings, Prop. 140 has brought new faces to Sacramento and has increased the ethnic and occupational diversity of our legislature. Those who worry that the quality of the legislature is diminished by the constant turnover have proposed that the limits be increased to twelve years per house (with an individual eligible for a total of twenty-four years if he or she wins a full measure of Assembly and Senate terms). Thus far, this change has proven too controversial to be enacted.

Redistricting and Gerrymandering: Drawing the Lines

Because legislators run from specific, numbered districts (eighty Assembly and forty State Senate), the political trend in each district is of critical importance to legislators. In order to keep population equal in each type of district, boundaries are redrawn every ten years (during the year following each Census), in a process known as *redistricting*. Lines for the state Assembly and Senate are decided by the legislators, who depend upon highly skilled demographers and political scientists to assist them. The legislature also has the responsibility to redraw California's congressional districts. Redistricting may involve a manipulation of boundaries (known as *gerrymandering*) to benefit particular individuals or groups or to increase the strength of whichever party has a majority in the legislature. Gerrymandering is highly political, with legislative committees devoting enormous time to partisan battling over district lines.

Because district lines are redrawn after each Census, legislative elections in November of Census years are particularly important to the major parties. In November 2000, the Republicans attempted, against the odds, to gain a majority, but the Democrats' head start was too much to overcome. With a 26–14 majority in the Senate and a 50–30 edge in the Assembly, Democrats hope to retain their majority for the entire decade by drawing many *safe districts* prior to the 2002 election. In safe districts, voter registration leans heavily toward one party, and no other party's candidate is likely to win the seat. However, with California's rapid demographic and related attitudinal changes, a safe district in 2002 may become increasingly *marginal* over time, and outcomes may become less predictable.

Legislative Functions and Procedures: How They Do Their Business

Unlike Congress, which has complete legislative power in the national government, the California legislature must share lawmaking authority with the voters through the initiative and referendum processes described earlier. Nonetheless, state government policy is set primarily by the legislature. In addition, it has the "power of the purse," levying taxes and appropriating money to finance the operation of all state agencies. After the passage of Prop. 13 (June 1978), the legislature provided a large percentage of local government revenue as well.

The legislature meets in two-year sessions. A bill introduced during the first year may continue to be considered during the second year without being reintroduced. When a bill is introduced, it moves slowly (with rare exceptions) through a complex process of committee hearings until it reaches the floor of the house where it began. Every bill must go through at least one committee, pass the full house, move through the second house's committee and floor, and then, finally, be sent to the governor. (Table 8.1 lists standing committees of the state Senate.) During this process, most bills are *amended*.

The powers of the Senate and Assembly are nearly identical, although only the approval of the Senate is needed to confirm certain administrative appointments by the governor. A member of either house can introduce any bill, and a majority of the entire membership of both houses is needed to pass most legislation. Figure 8.2 shows the procedure followed when a bill is introduced. A two-thirds majority is required for budget bills, proposed constitutional amendments, *overrides* of a veto and for urgency measures, which, unlike most laws, take effect immediately rather than on January 1 of the following year.

TABLE 8.1

Senate Standing Committees, 1999–2000

Agriculture and Water Resources	Housing and Community Developement
Appropriations	Industrial Relations
Budget and Fiscal Review	Insurance
Business and Professions	Judiciary
Constitutional Amendments	Legislative Ethics
Criminal Procedure	Local Government
Education	Natural Resources and Wildlife
Elections and Reapportionment	Public Employees and Retirement
Energy, Utilities and Communications	Revenue and Taxation
Environmental Quality	Rules
Finance, Investment and International Trade	Transportation
Governmental Organization	Veterans Affairs
Health and Human Services	

Source: California State Senate.

Presiding Officers: Each Party Gets Something

The lieutenant governor is the presiding officer, or president, of the Senate. In that capacity, however, he or she has little power and can vote only in cases of a tie. The person with greatest influence in the Senate is usually the *president pro tem* ("for a time"), a Senator elected as a substitute presiding officer by the entire Senate, and who becomes automatically the chair of the powerful Senate Rules Committee. The *pro tem* is almost always a member of the party with a majority of Senators. To counterbalance the pro tem's power, the minority caucus selects a minority leader to organize its work.

Like the Senate president pro tem, the speaker of the Assembly is elected by the entire body, but is typically a member of the majority party. The speaker is supposed to preside over the assembly, but often delegates the actual task to a speaker pro tem while the speaker "works the floor" (walks around lobbying the members). Once the most powerful legislator, the speaker's role has diminished since term limits make longevity in this role impossible. The minority party caucus elects its own floor leader as well as caucus chair.

Committees: Where the Real Work Gets Done

As in Congress, all members of the legislature serve on at least one *standing committee*. Most members of the Assembly serve on three committees and most Senators on four or five. Each bill that is introduced is referred to the appropriate committee and is considered by it in an order usually determined by the chairperson. Most bills that fail to become law are killed in committee; those enacted have often been amended there before being considered on the floor of the Senate or Assembly, where they may be further amended.

In marked contrast to the situation in Congress, committee chairs in the state legislature are not determined by seniority, and often include members of both parties. In the Senate, the power to organize committees and appoint their chairs and members is vested in the Rules Committee, made up of the president pro tem and four other Senators (two from each caucus). In addition to the Rules Committee, among the most important are the Education, Budget and Fiscal Review, Revenue and Taxation, Judiciary, and Health and Welfare committees.

In the Assembly, the speaker assigns most committees except for the Rules Committee. Among the most powerful is the Ways and Means Committee, which, like the Senate Budget and Fiscal Review Committee, considers all bills which involve state spending. Other important Assembly committees are the Insurance, Education, Agriculture, and Transportation committees.

If either house adds an amendment to a bill that is unacceptable to the house that first passed it, a *conference committee* consisting of three

Initial Steps by Author

Idea
Suggestions for legislation come from citizens, lobbyists, legislators, businesses, governor, and other public or private agencies.

Drafting
Formal copy of bill and brief summary are prepared by the Legislative Counsel.

Introduction
Bill is submitted by Senator or Assembly member, numbered and read for the first time; Rules Committee assigns bill to a committee. Printed. Action in house of origin.

Action in House of Origin

Committee
Once in committee, testimony is taken from author, proponents, and opponents. Bills can be passed, amended, held (killed), referred to another committee, or sent to interim study. Bills with a fiscal impact are referred to Appropriations Committee (Senate) and Ways and Means (Assembly).

Second Reading
Bills that pass out of committee are read a second time and placed on file for debate.

Floor Debate and Vote
Bills are read a third time and debated. A rollcall vote follows. For ordinary bills, a majority is needed to pass. For urgency bills and appropriation measures, a two-thirds majority is needed. Any member may seek reconsideration and another vote. If passed, the bill is sent to the second house.

FIGURE 8.2 **How a Bill Becomes Law in California.**
Source: Los Angeles County Almanac, 1991.

Senators and three Assembly members attempts to reach a compromise acceptable to both houses. When a bill is finally passed in the same form by both houses, it is sent to the governor for final action.

Loyalties in the Legislature: Party or Public?

The amount of partisanship in the legislature fluctuates. Both economic factors and personality help determine the mood of the legislature. During good times, the battles over how to spend tax dollars are less vicious than during times of cutbacks. Also, individual leadership styles impact the process. When less partisan people become leaders, they seek to reduce tensions between individuals and parties and seek compromise. Due to

Disposition in Second House

Reading
Bill is read for the first time and referred to a committee by the Assembly or Senate Rules Committee.

Committee
Procedures and possible actions are identical to those in the first house.

Second Reading
If approved, the bill is read a second time and placed on the daily file for debate and vote.

Floor Debate and Vote
As in the house of origin, recorded votes are taken after debate. If the bill is passed without having been further amended, it is sent to the governor's desk. (Resolutions are sent to the secretary of state.) If amended in the second house and passed, the measure returns to the house of origin for consideration of amendments.

Resolution of Two-House Differences

Concurrence
The house of origin decides whether to accept the other house's amendments. If approved, the bill is sent to the governor. If rejected, the bill is placed in the hands of a conference committee composed of three senators and three Assembly members.

Conference
If the conferees fail to agree, the bill dies. If the conferees present a recommendation for compromise (called a conference report), both houses vote on the report. If the report is adopted by both, the bill goes to the governor. If either house rejects the report, a second conference committee can be formed.

Role of the Governor

Sign or Veto?
Within 12 days after receiving a bill, the governor can sign it into law, allow it to become law without his signature, or veto it. A vetoed bill returns to the house of origin for possible vote on overriding the veto (requires a two-thirds majority of both houses). Urgency measures become effective immediately after signing. Others usually take effect the following January 1st.

FIGURE 8.2 (continued)

term limits, leaders rotate out quickly, and no one can rule the institution for fifteen years as did Democratic Speaker Willie Brown.

Although legislators are often criticized for placing petty concerns above the well-being of the public, the legislature as a body will continue to pass thousands of bills which, if signed by the governor, can affect all Californians. Just a few recent examples include laws to permit breast-feeding in public, to prevent doctors from referring patients to laboratories in which the doctor holds a financial interest, to require high school seniors to pass a state-approved test before graduating, to require convicted sex offenders to register upon release from custody, to create a new state Department of Managed Care which regulates health maintenance organizations (HMOs), to increase the marriage license fee to help finance domestic violence prevention programs, and to require children riding bicycles to wear safety helmets.

Questions to Consider

Using Your Text and Your Own Experiences

1. Define redistricting and gerrymander. How do the two concepts relate? Which word is more realistic to describe the process of redrawing political boundaries? Why?
2. What is your impression of California's legislative system? Is it efficient? Is it responsive to the public? If not, why not? How could the legislative process be improved?
3. How have term limits affected California's lawmaking process? Why do most lawmakers oppose term limits? What do you think of term limits and why?

Notes

1. Paul Jacobs, "Hill Convicted of Extortion in State Capitol Sting Case," *Los Angeles Times,* 17 June 1994, p. A1.
2. Jerry Gillam and Don Morain, "Citizens Panel Grants Legislators a 37% Raise," *Los Angeles Times,* 10 May 1994, p. A1.
3. Author interview with Mike Ward, Budget Officer of the California State Senate, 8 August 2000.

CHAPTER 9

The California Executive

"To create an enduring solution, an elected leader must find the most common ground possible among diverse groups."

Governor Gray Davis[1]

California voters elect eight statewide executive officials, of whom the governor is obviously the most important. The governor acts as the ceremonial head of state, representing it at various formal and informal functions, and has considerable influence over the selection of the chair of his or her party's state central committee. In the total system of checks and balances among the three branches of government, the governor exercises the executive checks. The most important of these is the *veto* power, especially when used on bills appropriating money.

The Veto Power and the Governor's Budget

When the legislature passes a bill, the governor has twelve days in which to veto it by sending it back to the legislature or to sign it into law. If he or she does neither, the bill becomes law automatically. The only time a governor gets more time is when the legislature goes into recess or adjourns and hundreds of bills may arrive in a few days. In this situation, the governor has thirty days to make decisions about bills. Governors vary in their eagerness to veto, and the frequency of the veto depends in part on whether the governor and the legislative majority are from the same party. If the legislative majority is from the other party, the governor may be sent many bills that are sure to be vetoed because of partisan conflicts or ideological differences. Only rarely can the legislature amass the two-thirds vote necessary to *override* a veto, so the governor's veto is a very powerful tool.

Each January the governor must send a budget bill to the legislature that provides for the expenditure of specified funds for all government agencies. Although the bill may be much amended before it is passed and returned to the governor in June, he or she may then use the *item veto*. This permits the deletion of a particular expenditure entirely or the reduction of its amount, thereby giving the governor major control over state spending.

Other Powers: Practical and Ceremonial

The governor's other checks on the legislative branch include sending messages to suggest new legislation and the authority to call special sessions. One of the more important ceremonial as well as political moments for a governor is the annual "State of the State" speech, given before the legislature and other constitutional officers in January. In this statement, the governor defines California's current situation and proposes legislative themes for the year. Ideas presented here can then be introduced as bills into the Assembly or Senate by the governor's allies in those bodies.

The governor's greatest influence on the judicial branch is the power to begin the careers of most judges by appointment (see Table 9.1 and the discussion of this procedure in the next chapter.) In addition, the governor may exercise *executive clemency*, which consists of pardons, commutations (reductions of sentences), and reprieves (postponements of sentences) granted to convicts. For those with past felony records, however, pardons and commutations require the approval of a majority on the state supreme court.

TABLE 9.1

Checks and Balances: The Governor's Appointments

Vacant Position	*Who Must Confirm Governor's Candidate*
Judicial: Appeals courts and state Supreme Court	Commission on Judicial Appointments
Judicial: Trial courts	No one (valid until next scheduled election)
U.S. Senate	No one (valid until next scheduled election)
County supervisor	No one (valid until next scheduled election)
Governor's personal staff	No one
Governor's cabinet	State Senate
Executive departments	State Senate
Boards and commissions	State Senate
Constitutional officers	State Senate and Assembly
Board of Equalization	State Senate and Assembly

Unusual Circumstances: Military and Police Powers

In times of emergency, the governor, as commander-in-chief of the California National Guard (unless the President has placed it under federal control), may call the guard into active duty. He or she may also direct the California Highway Patrol to bolster local police and sheriff's officers if intervention is needed on a smaller scale. Obviously, most governors prefer not to face natural disasters or human events that require the use of these powers.

Administrative Responsibility: The Power to Give Jobs

The governor enforces state laws through a vast administrative bureaucracy consisting of about fifty departments, most of which are currently grouped within five huge agencies: Business, Transportation and Housing, Health and Welfare, Resources, State and Consumer Services, and Youth and Adult Corrections. (See Figure 9.1.) The heads of these agencies, in addition to the directors of the Departments of Finance, Food and Agriculture, Industrial Relations, Trade and Commerce, Environmental Protection, Child Development and Education, and the Director of Information Technology, constitute the governor's cabinet and are appointed by the governor, subject to Senate confirmation. The finance director is responsible for preparing the entire state budget for submission to the legislature. In keeping with California's tradition of mistrust of political patronage, the governor actually appoints only 1 percent of the total state workforce, with the remaining state employees being civil servants.[2] However, those several hundred appointed jobs are at the highest levels of government and determine the functioning of virtually every state-run operation.

The governor also has the power to appoint members of many administrative boards, four of which are in the field of education. Appointments are made with the concurrence of the state Senate, and appointees are typically political supporters of the governor. Among these are the following:

1. The Board of Regents, which governs the nine campuses of the University of California (UC) and consists of eighteen members appointed by the governor for twelve-year terms, seven ex-officio members and one UC student who serves a one-year term
2. The Board of Trustees of the twenty-campus California State University system, composed of eighteen gubernatorial appointees who serve eight-year terms and five ex-officio members
3. The Board of Governors of the California Community Colleges, a sixteen-member group (including one faculty member) appointed by the governor for four-year terms to coordinate the seventy-two locally controlled community college districts

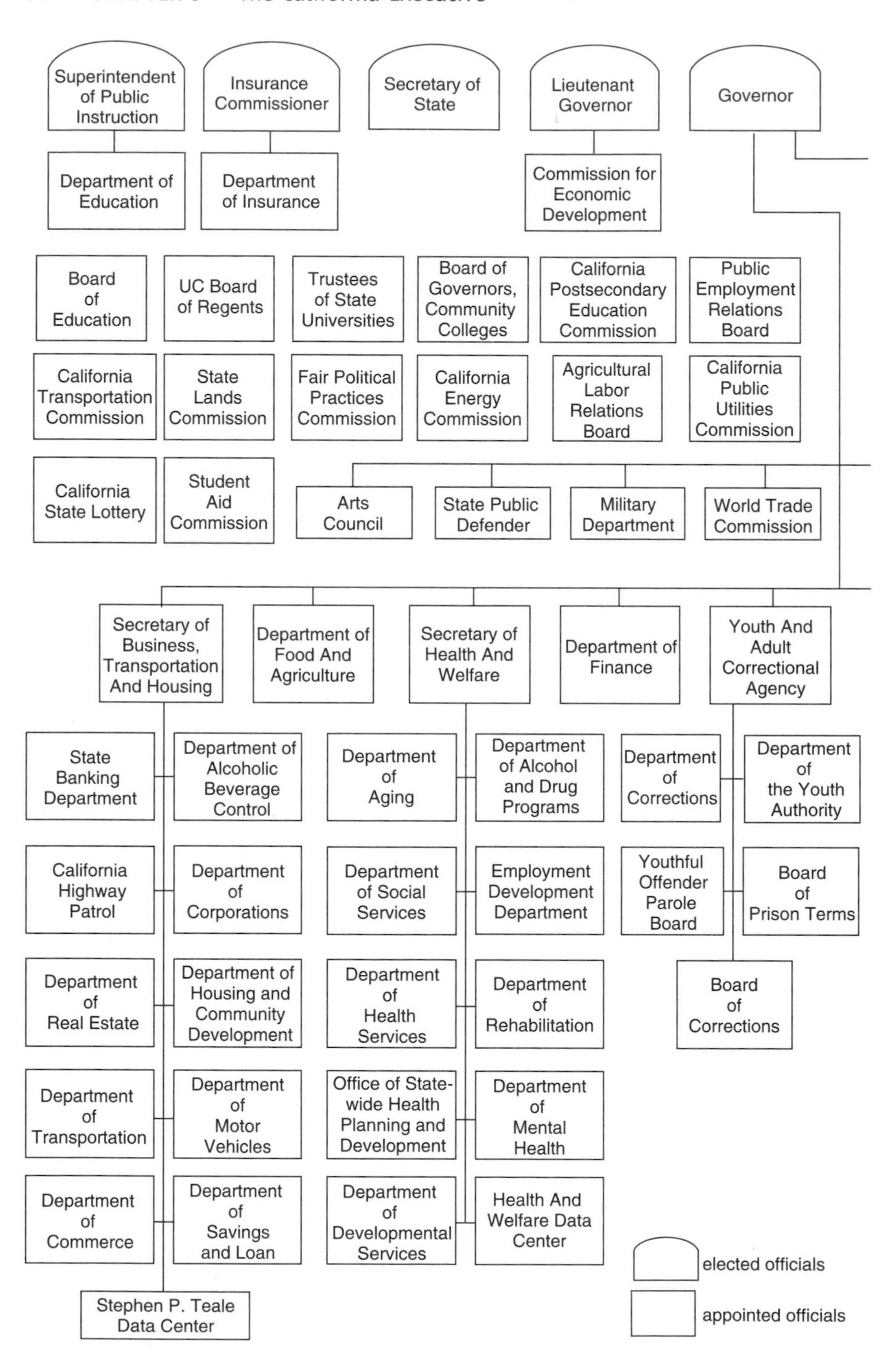

FIGURE 9.1 California State Government: The Executive Branch.

Source: League of Women Voters.

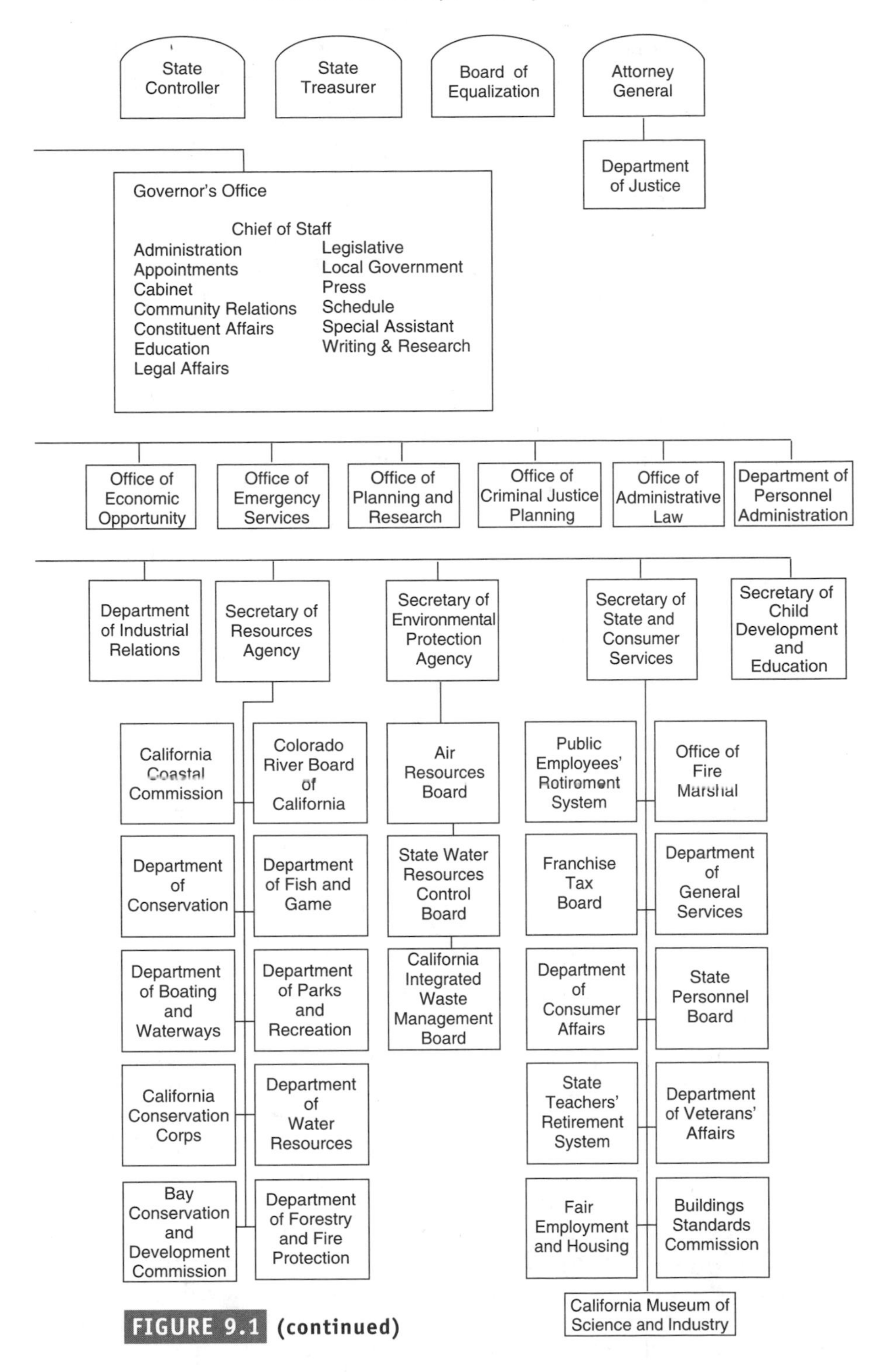

FIGURE 9.1 (continued)

4. The State Board of Education, the ten members of which are appointed for four-year terms to make policy for public schools throughout the state on such matters as curriculum and textbook selection
5. The five-member state Personnel Board, appointed for ten-year terms, which supervises the civil service system encompassing 98 percent of state employees
6. The five-person Public Utilities Commission, appointed for six-year terms, which licenses more than 1,500 privately owned companies and regulates the rates charged and services provided in the gas, water, telephone, telegraph, electricity, and transportation industries
7. The five-member Energy Commission, appointed for the purpose of coordinating energy needs and resources as well as promoting conservation and alternative technologies
8. The seven-member Fair Employment and Housing Commission, with responsibility for enforcing the laws against both job and housing discrimination
9. The Workers' Compensation Appeals Board, also consisting of seven members, which settles disputes regarding money paid to employees suffering job-related injuries or illness
10. The Board of Prison Terms, whose nine members determine which convicts should be granted parole from state prisons
11. The five-member Public Employment Relations Board, which regulates collective bargaining involving unions of workers employed by the state government and by public schools, colleges, and universities
12. The five-member Alcohol Beverage Control Board, which determines what alcohol licenses can be granted throughout the state

The politics of the appointment process are determined largely by the personal style of the governor. Governor Gray Davis has been committed to choosing moderate Democrats (and occasional Republicans) to fill the many positions under his authority. Opportunities to serve the Davis administration are publicized on his website, and Californians are encouraged to apply for positions throughout the executive branch. In order to ensure a unified perspective, he carefully evaluates and chooses his appointees. Many of Davis' fellow Democrats have felt impatient with his lengthy selection process, but there is little they can do to rush the governor. In the meantime, many "holdovers" from Pete Wilson's administration have continued to serve in key posts until their replacements are approved.

In addition to the many state boards and commissions the governor must fill, he or she also has the authority to appoint replacements to fill vacancies created by death or resignation on county boards of supervisors as well as those occurring for any of the seven other executive officers and for California's U.S. Senators. When former Insurance Commissioner Chuck Quackenbush resigned rather than face impeachment after allegedly funneling funds improperly, Governor Davis took the opportunity to replace him with a Democrat rather than another Republican. With so many responsibilities, California's governor is certainly comparable in importance to top corporate executives, yet the governor's salary is $156,000 per year, as compared to the multimillion-dollar salaries of most corporate leaders.

The Plural Executive: Training for Future Governors

In addition to the governor, seven other executive officials are elected directly by the voters. Like the governor, they are chosen for four-year terms (with a limit of two terms) and hold the following positions, often known as *constitutional offices.*

1. The lieutenant governor, in addition to being nominal president of the state Senate, succeeds to the governorship if that office becomes vacant between elections. The lieutenant governor also serves as acting governor when the governor is out of the state.

Due to the *office-block ballot,* with its emphasis on voting separately for each state office, Californians have often elected a governor from one party and a lieutenant governor from the other major party. This system, in which the second-in-command may be from a different party than the governor, has been criticized for promoting inefficiency and poor coordination between public officials. The Constitutional Revision Commission has urged that the governor and lieutenant governor run as a team, as the U.S. President and Vice-President do.[3] The current lieutenant governor, Cruz Bustamante, is a Democrat.

2. The attorney general, the chief legal adviser to all state agencies, is also head of the state Justice Department, which provides assistance to local law enforcement agencies, represents the state in lawsuits, and exercises supervision over the county district attorneys in their prosecution of state criminal defendants. This office is considered a prime position for future gubernatorial candidates, and Democrat Bill Lockyer is known to have gubernatorial ambitions.

3. The controller is concerned with government finance. He or she audits state expenditures, supervises financial restrictions on local governments, and influences state tax collections as a member of the Board of Equalization. Moreover, the controller has considerable patronage power in appointing inheritance tax appraisers and is a member of the State Lands Commission, which oversees the state's 4 million acres of public lands. He or she is also chair of the Franchise Tax Board, which collects income taxes. The office of controller, like that of attorney general, may also serve as a stepping stone to higher office. Democrat Kathleen Connell completes her second term in 2002.

4. The California secretary of state maintains official custody over state legal documents, grants charters to business corporations, and administers state election procedures. One of the most important tasks of the secretary of state is to verify the signatures on petitions for ballot initiatives, referendums, and recalls, and to administer state election laws.

Republican Bill Jones, known for creating a widely used Secretary of State website, reaches his term limit in 2002. He is the only Republican constitutional officer.

5. The state treasurer maintains custody over tax money collected by various state agencies, deposits it in private banks until appropriated by the legislature, sells government bonds, (presumably at the lowest possible interest rate), and influences stock investments by the public-employee pension funds. Democrat Phil Angelides, who can serve until 2006, has used his powers to change the investment policies of major state retirement systems so that they no longer invest in tobacco stocks.[4]

6. Perhaps the most controversial elected officer is the insurance commissioner. Until 1988, this was an appointed post. Then voters passed Prop. 103 and changed the position to an elected post in hopes that an elected commissioner would be more responsive to consumers. Instead, the most recent elected commissioner, Chuck Quackenbush, resigned amid accusations that he had abused his power to favor the insurance industry and promote his political ambitions. After he resigned, Governor Davis replaced Quackenbush with retired judge Harry Low, a Democrat, as the new commissioner until the 2002 election. Low is the highest-ranking Asian-American official in California.

7. The six executive officers listed above are, like the governor, nominated and elected through partisan campaigns. The superintendent of public instruction, however, is elected on a nonpartisan basis. The superintendent directs the state Department of Education and is charged with the responsibility for dispensing financial aid to local school districts, granting teaching credentials, and enforcing policies determined by the state Board of Education. In addition, the superintendent is an *ex-officio* member of the UC Board of Regents and the California State University Board of Trustees. Delaine Eastin, a Democrat backed by teacher groups across the state, will reach her term limit in 2002.

In addition to the constitutional executive officers just mentioned, California voters choose four members of the Board of Equalization from the four districts into which the state is divided for this purpose. This board collects the sales tax, a major source of state revenue, and equalizes the basis on which local property taxes are assessed by the fifty-eight county assessors in California.

Although the executive branch, including its many agencies, appears large and perhaps excessively layered with bureaucracy, California has been cited as the state with "the most efficient use of bureaucrats" because it employs only 5.75 state workers for every 1,000 Californians.[5]

Despite this positive assessment of the state's bureaucracy, the election of so many executive officials is frequently criticized. The voters have little information about the candidates seeking these offices, and the governor cannot coordinate their activities effectively. This problem is particularly acute when some of the constitutional officers are not of the governor's party or are even potential future rivals for the governorship.

However, despite suggestions from the Constitutional Revision Commission to reduce the number of elected executive officers (and replace them with appointees),[6] there is little indication that the structure at the top will change soon.

Questions to Consider

Using Your Text and Your Own Experiences

1. Describe some of the governor's powers. Which ones are most important (i.e., affect large numbers of people and are used frequently)? Which ones does a governor prefer not to use?
2. Discuss the governor's powers to appoint other officials. How does this power help shape the everyday lives of Californians? Give specific examples.
3. What is the relationship between the governor and the legislature? What checks and balances are built into the California constitution for these two branches of government?

Notes

1. Gray Davis, "Getting the Ball Rolling: Leadership and Momentum," *CORO Leadership Review,* June 2000, p. 79.
2. Bradley Inman, "Many Are Calling but Few Will Be Chosen," *Los Angeles Times,* March 17, 1991, p. D2.
3. California Constitution Revision Commission, Final Report and Recommendations to the Governor and the Legislature, 1996, p. 3.
4. Marjorie Kelly, "SRI is Popping up Everywhere in California," *Business Ethics,* March/April 2000, p. 2.
5. Dan Miller, "States' Numbers Say It All," *City and State,* 23 April 1990, p. 14.
6. Final Report and Recommendations to the Governor and the Legislature from the Constitutional Revision Commission, Sacramento, 1996, p. 18.

CHAPTER 10
The California Courts

"Without confidence in a fair and accessible judicial system, young people are less likely to grow up as law-abiding citizens."

Ron George, Chief Justice of the California State Supreme Court

Unlike the federal system, in which judges are appointed by the President, confirmed by the Senate, and serve for life with no further review, the state's system involves a complicated combination of appointments and elections for judges. This complex system classifies judges into two categories: trial-court judges and appeals judges. The judges and their courts serve the largest population in the nation, cost approximately $2 billion per year to run, and receive nearly two-thirds of that money from the state.[1] They deal with over 8 million civil and criminal cases per year.[2] Recent reorganizations of the courts have improved services by reducing backlogs of cases awaiting trial while exploring new options such as special drug treatment courts, faster adoption procedures, and increased legal assistance for low-income Californians. Additional new programs include the use of mediation rather than court trials to resolve family disputes and other civil matters, and special courts for the homeless.[3]

Combining Courts: California's New Trial Court System

As a result of Prop. 220 (1998), California developed an option for merging the municipal and Superior Court systems in each county. As of 2001, every one of the fifty–eight counties has now combined the municipal courts with the Superior Court structure. This unification of courts was designed to improve efficiency and reduce the waiting time for court trials. All of the duties of the trial courts are now assigned to superior courts, including criminal trials, juvenile dependency, civil lawsuits, and all aspects of family law. Superior court judges earn $127,935 per year, and in some counties are assisted by court commissioners who can perform many of the functions of the judges. Despite the recent consolidation, efficiency has not been the hallmark of the trial court system, and much remains to be accomplished in order to provide speedy justice to Californians.

Alternatives to the Courts: Buying Judicial Services

Due to the overcrowded and often-delayed court system, Californians, sometimes unwillingly, have turned to private arbitrators to resolve their civil differences. Many Californians do not realize that when they accept many job opportunities or join most health insurance plans they must sign a binding arbitration clause which denies them the right to sue in court and, instead, requires them to go to binding (no-appeals) arbitration to resolve disputes with the employer or insurer. Private arbitration is different from mediation in that mediation is used to resolve issues outside of court, but mediation does not include a "no-appeals" agreement. Private arbitrators, often retired judges, have been criticized for having excessive power, since their decisions are not appealable. With continuing reforms, arbitration remains a useful tool when both sides in a lawsuit agree to use private judges, because it can save time if the parties are willing and able to pay for their "day in court."

Where Appeal Rights Remain Intact: District Courts in Action

For those who cannot afford or do not wish to use private alternatives, one advantage of using local trial courts to resolve legal problems is the right to appeal. When an individual believes that a lower court has made a legal error in deciding a case, he or she may appeal—if financial resources are available to do so. California is divided into six court of appeal districts, headquartered in San Francisco, Los Angeles, Sacramento, Fresno, San Jose, and San Diego. Three judges consider each case, with a total of 93 judges earning $146,404 each. The appeals courts continue to see a heavy workload in the areas of juvenile cases, civil cases, and criminal cases.

California Supreme Court: The Last Resort (Almost)

Most of the state Supreme Court's work is handling appeals passed up from the appellate courts. The only cases that come to this court directly are requests from death-row prisoners asking the court to review their sentence. It consists of a chief justice, now Ronald M. George, who receives $163,767, and six associate justices, who earn $156,162. If an individual involved in a case at this level is still not satisfied, he or she may choose to appeal to the U.S. Supreme Court. However, cases which raise constitutional questions appropriate to the U.S. Supreme Court are rare, and the state Supreme Court is the final court of appeal for most cases it determines.

The Selection of Judges: A Mix of Politics and Performance

Although trial court judges are chosen by the voters in nonpartisan elections for six-year terms, in reality, few judges begin their careers by running for office. Most judgeships are initially filled because there is a vacancy due to death, retirement, or the creation of new judgeships by the legislature. These vacancies are filled by the governor. The only constitutional requirement to become a trial court judge is to have been a lawyer in California for at least ten years; however, the Governor's "short list" will typically include attorneys who have some political connections. Once appointed, the new judge serves until the next election, at which time these incumbents have the advantage. Although attorneys are entitled to run against trial court judges, challengers rarely emerge, so the elections are usually canceled. Since there are no term limits for judges, those willing to work for public salaries (generally much lower than salaries of private attorneys) can easily sustain a judicial career in California for decades without their names ever appearing on a ballot.

In contrast, for the higher courts, all judges' names eventually appear on the ballot. Appeals court judges and Supreme Court justices are chosen by a method which enhances gubernatorial power to influence the judiciary. The three-step process includes:

1. Appointment by the governor.
2. Approval by the Commission on Judicial Appointments, which consists of a Supreme Court justice, a district Court of Appeals justice and the state attorney general.
3. Election (confirmation) for a twelve-year term, with no opposing candidate permitted to run and voters limited to a choice between "yes" and "no." There are no term limits for judges.

In making judicial appointments at all levels (see Figure 10.1), governors usually give special consideration to attorneys who have supported them in their political campaigns and who have a good rating from the state Bar Association. In addition, just as the President can use judicial appointments to promote his or her agenda in the federal system, the political views of the governor have an enormous impact on the types of judges appointed. Governor Gray Davis has made clear that all his judicial

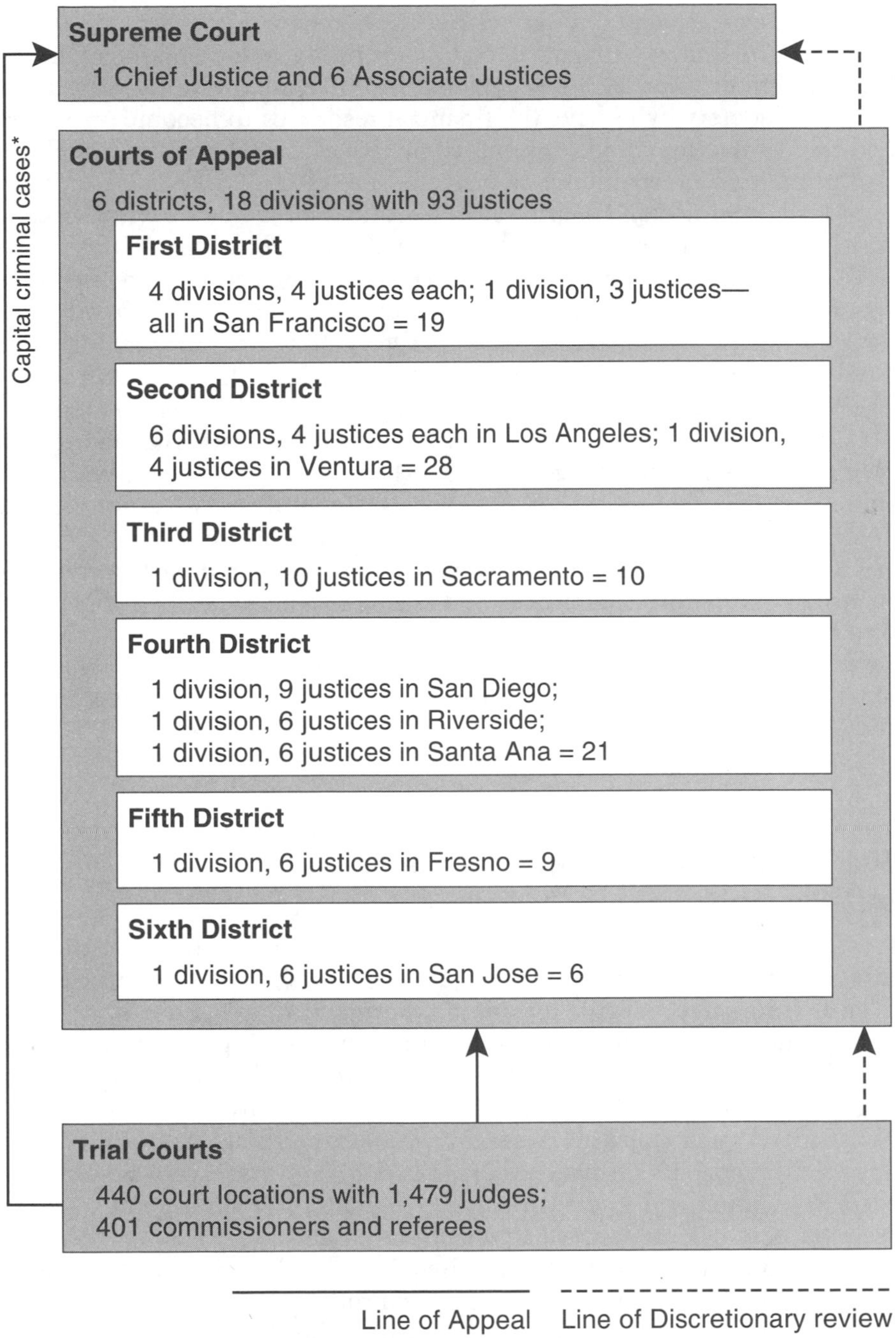

Supreme Court

1 Chief Justice and 6 Associate Justices

Capital criminal cases*

Courts of Appeal

6 districts, 18 divisions with 93 justices

First District

4 divisions, 4 justices each; 1 division, 3 justices—
all in San Francisco = 19

Second District

6 divisions, 4 justices each in Los Angeles; 1 division,
4 justices in Ventura = 28

Third District

1 division, 10 justices in Sacramento = 10

Fourth District

1 division, 9 justices in San Diego;
1 division, 6 justices in Riverside;
1 division, 6 justices in Santa Ana = 21

Fifth District

1 division, 6 justices in Fresno = 9

Sixth District

1 division, 6 justices in San Jose = 6

Trial Courts

440 court locations with 1,479 judges;
401 commissioners and referees

Line of Appeal — Line of Discretionary review

FIGURE 10.1 California Court System.

*Death penalty cases are automatically appealed from the superior court directly to the Supreme Court.

Source: California State Constitution.

appointees are expected to reflect his views on issues such as the death penalty (pro) and gay marriage (con). Depending upon who is governor, judicial appointments generally tend to represent the more privileged groups in society (who have the financial resources to become attorneys and the connections to be nominated by the governor) and do not reflect the ethnic or socioeconomic diversity of the state.

Once appointed and confirmed, few justices have trouble winning confirmation from the voters. With the unusual exception of the "Dump Rose Bird" campaign of the mid–1980s, neither voters nor election strategists have spent much time worrying about who sits on the California courts. Rose Bird, appointed by Democratic Governor Jerry Brown to the state Supreme Court despite her lack of judicial experience, became the symbol of "soft" liberalism regarding capital punishment. The successful campaign to unseat her also resulted in the voters' removal of two other justices appointed by Democratic governors, allegedly for also being too "soft" on crime. When these three liberal justices lost their posts, Republican Governor George Deukmejian replaced them with three conservative justices.

Since then, voters have returned to a more normal pattern of confirming gubernatorial nominees and keeping most incumbent judges in office. With rare exceptions, interest in judicial contests is low, and voters often feel that they are casting a ballot "blindly" when they vote on judges. Few Californians pay attention to the quality of their judges until they need to appear in court and see a judge in action.

The Nonelectoral Removal of Judges: Rare but Possible

In order to have another avenue by which to remove judges, the Commission on Judicial Performance is a group which can force out a judge even if voters have elected him or her. Formed in 1961, the commission is now made up of three judges appointed by the Supreme Court, two members of the state Bar Association appointed by the governor, and two nonlawyer members chosen by the governor, two by the Senate Rules Committee, and two by the Assembly Speaker, creating a total of six nonlawyer members. Its primary task is to investigate complaints about judicial misconduct and, if circumstances indicate, to recommend that the state Supreme Court remove a judge from office.

The commission receives hundreds of complaints each year about judges. Misconduct charges that may be brought against judges include accusations of racial or gender bias, substance abuse, verbal abuse, accepting bribes, personal favoritism, and even senility. In 1994, through Prop. 190, voters established new guidelines for the commission, including the requirement that judicial performance proceedings be opened to the public.[4] However, judges are rarely removed from the bench, and only a handful have ever been disciplined by the commission.

The Judicial Council: Running a Complex System

The twenty-one voting members of the Judicial Council are empowered to evaluate and improve the administration of justice in the state. Made up of judges, attorneys, and legislative appointees, the council analyzes the workloads of the courts, recommends reorganizations to improve efficiency, and establishes many of the rules of court procedure. Its recommendations may become the basis for legislative decisions to expand or restructure the judicial branch.

Judicial Power: Who Has It and How They Use It

While judges at the local level do not permanently affect questions of constitutionality nor set policy through their decisions, the appellate justices and state Supreme Court justices can create legal precedents for California through their written decisions. Because they wield such power, governors should choose justices carefully. However, governors have their own political preferences. They realize that a judgeship will probably last much longer than their term as governor, and they select justices whose overall political views are compatible with their own, expecting these justices to make legal decisions which meet their political goals. Of course, over time, some appointees disappoint the governors who put them there, by making decisions contrary to the wishes of their "patrons."

Six of the seven current members of the state Supreme Court were appointed by Republican governors. None of the seven has served as a public defender, civil rights lawyer, labor lawyer, or academic. Most of them come from a background of business-oriented law, and their rulings reflect those biases.[5] They are a relatively youthful group and could easily remain on the high court for several decades into the new century. Three of the seven are women, and the court is ethnically diverse, with Asian-American, Latino, and African-American justices. As it is currently constituted, the state's highest court can be expected to continue on a pragmatic course for the foreseeable future, and Governor Davis' first appointment to the court reinforced that middle-of-the-road approach.

Although individuals who have been in California courtrooms and seen judicial authority in action may feel intimidated or powerless, the public must remember that its electoral choice for governor determines the tone of the judicial branch. If one wants liberal judges, one must elect liberal governors, and the same is true for conservatives. If one wants more women and ethnic minorities represented on the bench, one must evaluate the records and promises of gubernatorial candidates regarding judicial appointments. Likewise, if one believes that justice is colorblind, one must try to elect a candidate who promises to select judges without regard to gender or ethnicity. The important element is the citizen's awareness of the connection between voting for governor and the quality of justice in California.

awareness of the connection between voting for governor and the quality of justice in California.

Questions to Consider

Using Your Text and Your Own Experiences

1. Compare and contrast the federal judicial system with California's judicial branch in terms of how judges are selected, their length of service, etc.
2. What is the role of the governor in the judicial branch? Does the governor have too much power? How do voters get involved in judicial decision making?
3. Debate the pros and cons of California's judicial confirmation elections. Is judicial independence compromised by this system?

Notes

1. "Foundations for a New Century," Judicial Council of California, Administrative Office of the Courts, 2000 Court Statistics Report, (available at www.courtinfo.ca.gov).
2. Ibid.
3. Tony Perry, "Homeless Court Offers New Hope for the Down and Out," *Los Angeles Times,* 22 May 2000, p. A3.
4. *League of Women Voters State Ballot Measures,* Sacramento, September 12, 1994, p. 7.
5. Bob Egelko, "A Low Profile Court," *California Journal,* June 1994, p. 38.

CHAPTER 11

Criminal Justice and Civil Law

"We've created 10,000 new jobs in the prison system and financed those jobs by cutting 10,000 positions out of the university and state college system."
Bill Lockyer, Attorney General

All the vast machinery of the judicial system and its related components, including the judges, attorneys, bailiffs, stenographers, police, jails, wardens, and parole officers (to name a few), serves to facilitate two basic types of legal procedures: civil litigation and criminal prosecutions. Although many Californians' maximum contact with the entire judicial/legal system is their occasional jury duty, for others their lives are profoundly affected by the structures and processes of the criminal justice system and/or the civil courts.

Criminal Justice: An Oxymoron?

Depending on the severity of the act, crimes are normally defined as felonies, misdemeanors, or infractions. *Infractions* are most often violations of traffic laws, while *misdemeanors* encompass the "less serious" crimes such as shoplifting and public drunkenness. *Felonies*, the most serious crimes and potentially punishable by a year or more in state prison, include both violent and nonviolent crimes.

Although crime rates in the state have gone down in recent years, Californians continue to show concern about protecting themselves from criminals. Law enforcement and researchers disagree about the impact of the "three-strikes" law, with law enforcement claiming success in reducing crime rates but critics pointing out that nonviolent felons are being sentenced to life at a cost to taxpayers of $500,000 to $1 million per inmate.[1] Since the law's passage in 1994, despite a multimillion-dollar prison construction program, California's prisons remain tremendously overcrowded, with periodic outbreaks of violence—in some cases involving accusations that prison guards instigated the trouble. Private prison contractors are attempting to convince lawmakers that they should build and run prisons, but the powerful California Correctional Peace Officers Association (CCPOA) adamantly opposes *privatization*.[2] Table 11.1 lists statistics about the California Department of Corrections.

Crime and Its Victims: Technology Advances, Fears Remain

Even during relative prosperity, California has its share of unemployment, family instability, mental illness, and ignorance—the underlying causes of much of the crime committed. Public fears of violent crime have lead to a series of ballot initiatives, including Prop. 21 (2000), which requires juveniles aged fourteen or older to be tried as adults for murder and increases penalties for gang-related offenses. Crimes committed by adults are decreasing, while juvenile crime rates continue to increase, fueling concerns that prevention programs involving jobs and education are not funded adequately.[3]

Californians worried about violent crime do not necessarily agree on solutions. While opinion polls repeatedly indicate that a large majority support gun controls, the vocal minority of gun rights supporters continues to lobby against any restrictions. Communities plagued by crime have tried everything from forming Neighborhood Watch com-

TABLE 11.1

California Department of Corrections, 1997

Budget	$4.6 billion
Average yearly cost	$21,470 per inmate
	$2,145 per parolee
Staff	44,976 in institutions, parole, and administration
Facilities	33 state prisons
	38 wilderness area camps
	8 prisoner mother facilities
Inmate population	160,846 (200% of capacity)
	93% male, 7% female
	34% Hispanic, 31% black, 30% white, 6% other
Offense	43% violent crime
	23% property crime
	28% drugs
	6% other
Condemned to death	564

Source: California Department of Corrections, available from http://www.cdc.state.ca.us/factsht.html

mittees, which try to link neighbors in a network of alert watchfulness, to demanding speed bumps and private gates. Some local governments have responded by initiating "community policing," a system designed to improve communication between neighborhoods and their police force.[4] Unfortunately, the responsiveness of government agencies sometimes depends on a community's political clout. In low-income areas with little political influence, residents often feel neglected by public safety agencies and do not have the money to purchase alternative sources of protection. More affluent communities have the funds to build gates and walls as well as to hire private security companies to patrol their streets. But everyone, rich and poor alike, tends to become cynical when local public law enforcement agencies are found to be corrupt, and officers of the law, such as those from the Ramparts Division of the Los Angeles Police Department (LAPD), are found guilty of abusing their authority.

Because of immense public fears about violent crime, less attention is paid to some of the more subtle white-collar crimes. Whether the economy is at boom or bust, con artists and hucksters can cause irreparable harm. Californians have been cheated out of millions by pyramid investment schemes, phony mortgage loans, fraudulent land sales, staged auto accidents, and other illegal and unethical ways to part people from their money. While most white-collar crime is nonviolent, sometimes auto insurance scam artists cause innocent people to die when they create accidents in order to file lawsuits. Victims of white-collar crime are often elderly, immigrants, or uneducated.

Even though statistics say that crime is down, the most utilized form of the media, television, continues to focus on lurid, violent crime as a mechanism to attract viewers, leaving people with the sense that they could at any moment become victims of random savagery and that political leaders must do something about it. Since much of violent crime is linked to drug abuse, illegal drug dealing, and domestic violence, the courts are experimenting with "collaborative courts" which involve treatment providers and close monitoring of offenders.[5] In response to the increasing sense that rehabilitation must be part of the solution to drug abuse, voters passed Prop. 36 (2000) which calls for treatment rather than prison time for non-violent drug offenders. Some politicians continue to remind the public that it costs taxpayers about $22,000 per year to keep someone in prison,[6] while the state currently spends about $7,793 on a public school child and $4,000 on a community college student.

The Criminal Justice Process: A System to Avoid

In many cases, crimes occur and are not reported, or they are reported but no suspect is arrested. In the cases where an arrest is made, the arresting officer often has the option of "naming" the crime by labeling it either a misdemeanor or a felony. If a person is arrested for a felony, the county district attorney's office must then decide whether to file the felony charge. In cases without witnesses willing to testify, filing charges becomes a dicey proposition in which tax dollars may be spent on a trial only to arrive at an inconclusive outcome. Due to the strength of some gangs, witnesses are often afraid to testify against someone who could take revenge on the witness or a family member.

Under federal Constitutional rights, persons accused of crimes are entitled to speedy trials. With the number of felony trials rising 144 percent since 1979,[8] courts must seek ways to reduce their load. *Plea bargains*, in which the accused person's defense attorney can cut a "deal" with prosecutors and receive a reduced sentence in exchange for eliminating a trial, continue to be common. Defendants with adequate funds may be represented by a private attorney; however, most accused persons must rely on overworked public defenders to handle their cases. Trials may be decided by either a judge or a jury, depending on the preference of the defendant and his or her attorney. If a jury is used, the entire jury must agree on the final verdict of guilty or not, while the judge determines the sentence. The sole exception to this rule is in capital (death penalty) cases, in which the jury, again by unanimous vote, has the duty to recommend either the death penalty or life in prison. (Figure 11.1 shows the locations of prisons in the California system.)

Civil Law: Solving Problems Through the Courts

While criminal law deals with matters which are considered injurious to the "people of the state of California," civil matters involve any disputes between parties which cannot be resolved without legal assistance. Parties involved in such disputes can include individuals, business entities, and government agencies. The range of civil legal matters includes such cases as dissolution of marriage, child custody, personal injury (including automobile accidents), malpractice, workers' compensation, breach of contract, bankruptcy, and many more. In these cases, the court's role frequently is to determine liability and to assess damages, often amounting to hundreds of thousands of dollars.

Most civil lawsuits never reach a court. Those that do go to trial may be decided by a judge or a jury, with only a three-quarters majority of jurors required to agree in order to decide the outcome. Because civil cases have no Constitutional protection against delay, waiting for a court date can sometimes last years. One way to avoid the delay is an out-of-court settlement arranged by the attorneys of the parties involved. These settlements often save time, money, and aggravation for both the *plaintiff* and the *defendant*. Another alternative to the long wait is to pay private arbitrators (often retired judges) to settle disputes outside the public judicial system. However, both parties must agree to accept the arbitrator's decision. This *privatization* of the civil legal system may result in speedier

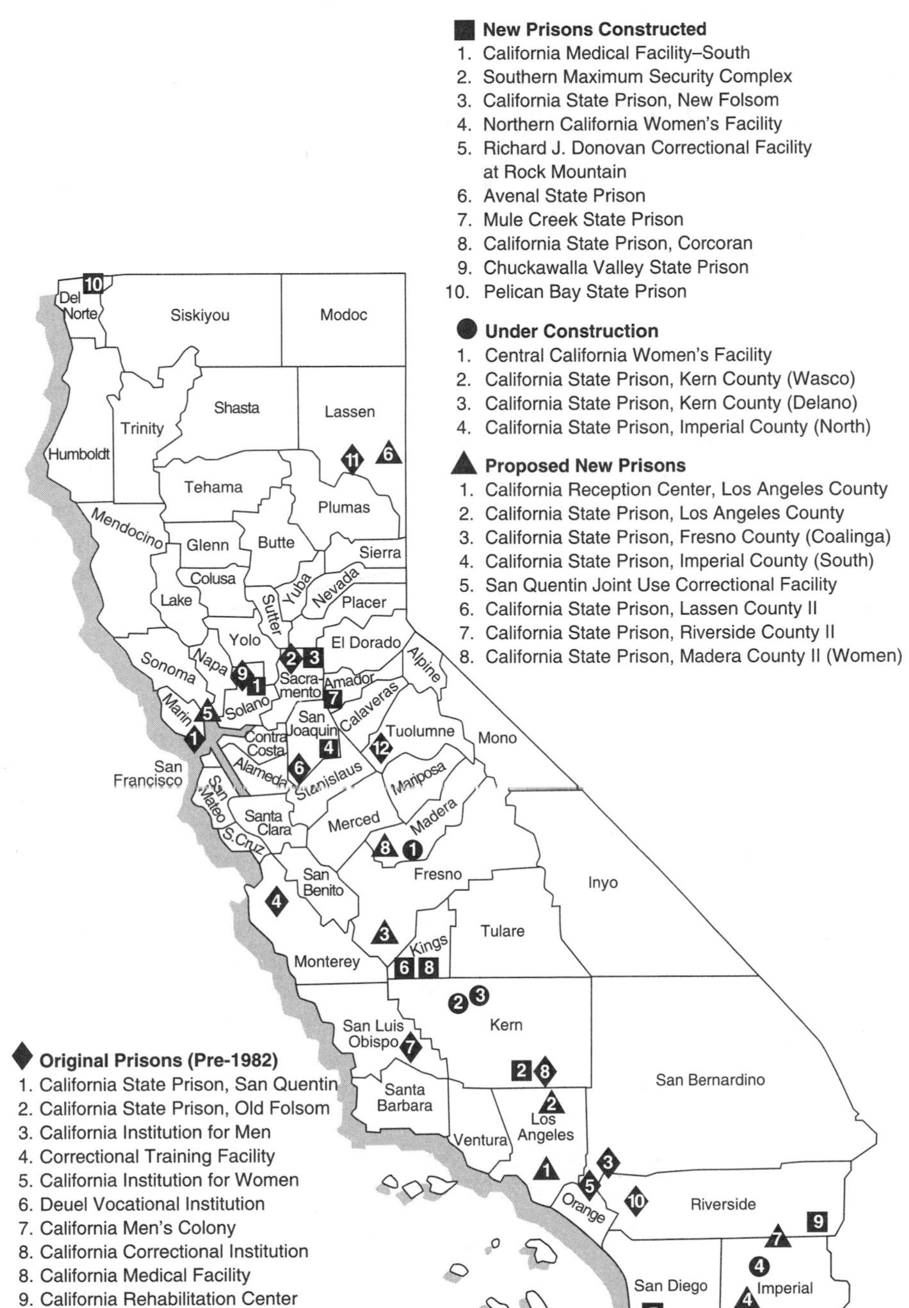

FIGURE 11.1 Californai State Prisons.

Source: Department of Corrections.

justice for those able to buy an arbitrator's time while those involved in the public system continue to wait years for their case to come to court.

Juries: The Citizen's Duty

California has two types of juries, the most common being the trial jury and the less known type being the grand jury. In both cases, jurors must be U.S. citizens. The county grand jury, made up of a select group of citizens nominated by Superior Court judges, serves a one-year term for minimal compensation, thus leaving this task to the affluent or retired. Their original purpose was to investigate any possible misconduct in local government and to return *indictments*, or charges, against officials who may have abused their powers. Since Prop. 115 (1990), their secondary function of indicting criminals outside of government has been emphasized to the point that many grand juries have become so busy dealing with criminal matters that they do not have enough time to investigate public officials.[9]

Unlike the grand jury selected for a year, trial juries are created for the length of a particular trial. For felony trials, the jury is composed of twelve citizens, while as few as nine jurors may try a misdemeanor case or a civil trial. Trial juries are found through both voter registration and motor vehicle license lists. County courts send out notices asking citizens to serve, and penalties for failure to respond have increased to $1,500 in some counties. Those with reasonable explanations can be excused from jury duty; these legitimate reasons include economic hardship, child-care problems for those with small children, and serious illness.

The jury system has been criticized for many reasons, including the low compensation ($15 per day), the potential for emotional (rather than rational) decision making, and the poor use of jurors' time when they do agree to serve. Recent efforts to improve the situation include the one-day-or-one-trial system (which allows people to get back to work more quickly), the use of pager and call-in systems to avoid long waits, and improved jury waiting areas. Although jury duty is often perceived as a boring chore, the jury system is still considered one of the genuine advantages of living in a democratic society with a Constitutional right to "an impartial jury" and "due process of law."[10]

Questions to Consider

Using Your Text and Your Own Experiences

1. What are some of the root causes of our overloaded criminal justice system? What can be done about solving them?
2. What are some alternatives to our overloaded civil courts? How else can problems be resolved between individuals or organizations?

3. What could be done to increase the number of people who serve on juries? Share your experiences, if any, doing jury duty.

Notes

1. Greg Krikorian, "Three Strikes Law Has No Effect, Study Finds," *Los Angeles Timesp* 2 March 1999, p. A3.
2. Noel Brinkerhoff, "Lock 'Em Up?," *California Journal,* February 1999, pp. 9–16.
3. Anne Hendershott, "Juvenile Delinquency and Urban Gangs in California," in Charles F. Hohm, ed., *California's Social Problems,* Addison Wesley Longman, 1997, pp. 99–113.
4. Huntington Beach Police Department document, "Community Policing," Spring 1994.
5. Ronald M. George, Chief Justice of the California Supreme Court, State of the Judiciary Address, March 28, 2000.
6. California Department of Corrections Facts," 1 August 1997, http://www.cdc.state.ca.us/factsht.html.
7. "Focus on Crime and Drug Policy," *Rand Research Review,* Vol. XIX, No. 1, Spring 1995.
8. "Foundations for a New Century," Judicial Council of California, Administrative Office of the Courts, 1999, p. 7.
9. Bill Boyarsky, "The Watchdog with Scant Time to Watch," *Los Angeles Times,* May 11, 1994, p. B3.
10. Amendments V and VI, U.S. Constitution.

CHAPTER 12
City Governments

"The power of local governments to make choices about the level and quality of local services has eroded over the last 20 years. Local communities should be given more local control."

Constitutional Revision Commission, 1996

There are three types of local government in California—counties, cities, and special districts (including school districts), plus regional agencies that attempt to coordinate their policies. Of these, city government is probably the level of local government most accessible to the public. Cities have enormous responsibilities to their residents, but are severely constrained by budget limitations, especially the loss of local property tax revenues caused by Prop. 13. Like other levels of government, finding the best ways to generate revenues and provide needed services is an ongoing battle among city officials.

How Cities Are Created: It's Not Easy

With the exceptions of some of the older cities, such as Los Angeles, San Francisco, and San Jose, which received their charters from the state when California was admitted to the Union, most cities in California "incorporate" when the residents decide they need their own local government. Prior to incorporation, areas which are not cities are called *unincorporated areas,* and their residents normally receive basic urban services from the county in which they live. Occasionally, an unincorporated area is simply annexed, or joined with, a nearby city by a majority vote of that territory's residents along with the approval of the adjacent city.

Perhaps the most common reason why residents initiate the incorporation process is that the county government, which provides their services, is too far away and unresponsive. If residents feel that police and fire protection is inadequate, or that planning and zoning issues are not well handled, or even that rents are too high in the area, they may organize to create their own city in which they can elect their own officials to control these issues. Of course, residents who want their own city government must realize that there are costs involved in running a city, and they must be prepared to tax themselves to pay for city services. They must also agree to share their tax revenues with the county so it can maintain its county-wide services to their residents.[1]

Incorporation begins with a petition signed by at least 25 percent of the registered voters in an area. The petition is then submitted to the *Local Agency Formation Commission* (LAFCO). Each county has a LAFCO to analyze all issues relating to incorporation, boundary changes, and annexations. The LAFCO must determine the economic feasibility of a proposed city. If the LAFCO decides that cityhood would be financially viable, it authorizes an election in which cityhood can be approved by a simple majority.

In a more recent development, the concept of cities breaking up has become hotly debated, especially in the city of Los Angeles, where citizens of the Hollywood, San Pedro, and San Fernando Valley areas have submitted petitions to secede. Residents complain of lack of attention and resources from City Hall, and propose creating new, independent cities. However, due to intricate financial issues, the process of *secession* has yet to produce a new city in California.

City Responsibilities: Many Tasks, Limited Revenues

Whether a city is a "general law" city which derives all its powers from statutes passed by the state legislature, or a "charter" city which has its own locally written constitution, all cities share similar tasks and responsibilities. Basic, day-to-day necessities such as sewage and garbage disposal, police and fire protection, libraries, streets and traffic control, recreation and parks facilities, and planning and zoning policy form the backbone of city services. In many cities, some of these services are provided through contracts with the county to purchase services such as law enforcement, fire protection, and street maintenance.

Until 1978, cities obtained about one-fourth of their revenues from local property taxes. After Prop. 13 slashed this source, cities cut back many services and turned to the state capital in Sacramento for assistance. However, Sacramento does not provide resources comparable to those lost from local property taxes. To fill in the budget gaps, most cities now rely on utility and sales taxes, as well as an array of increased fees, including those for building permits, recreational facilities, real estate transfers, garbage collection, and more. Business licenses, parking taxes, traffic fines, and limited federal grants are additional sources of revenue. Since the passage of Prop. 218 (1996), voters are required to authorize many local taxes which have existed for years, and politicians must now make the case for taxes in order to get support at the ballot box.

Despite their relatively diverse funding sources, few cities enjoy the luxury of being able to spend freely, and most city governments spend a great deal of time deciding how best to allocate the scarce resources available. Police departments usually obtain the largest chunk of city monies, leaving fire services, libraries, parks and recreation, and other departments to battle for their share of the pie.

Forms of City Government: Two Basics with Variations

Although there are numerous local versions, city government in California falls within two broad types. The *mayor–council* variety entails a separation of powers between the mayor, who has executive responsibility for the functioning of most city departments, and the council, which enacts legislation known as *ordinances*. If the mayor has the power to veto ordinances and to appoint department heads, the government is known as a strong mayor–council variety; if not, it is a weak mayor–council system. Larger cities sometimes include aspects of both the "strong" and "weak" systems. (Figure 12.1 shows the city council districts of Los Angeles.)

The *council–manager* type of government gives the city council both executive and legislative power, but the council exercises its executive power by appointing a professionally trained city manager to coordinate and administer city departments. These city managers are usually very well paid (many earn more than the state's governor) and serve as long as the council wishes. In this form of government, there is a ceremonial mayor with no executive powers, who is merely one of the council members. This mayoral position is typically rotated around the council, with each member serving a year and then returning to his or her regular council status. The mayor continues to hold a vote equal to that of every other member of the city council.

Los Angeles and San Francisco employ the mayor–council form, while Oakland, San Jose, and Torrance are among the 90 percent of all cities in the state that use the council–manager form.[2] Under either system, most cities have a city clerk, attorney, treasurer or controller, and planning commission, with all but the latter elected directly by voters. The most common departments are police, fire, public works, recreation and parks, and building. These are usually headed by high-level civil servants and monitored by advisory commissions appointed by elected officials.

While access to city bureaucracies depends in part on the size of the city, a resident with a complaint about city services had best do his or her homework regarding the structure of city government in order to get the fastest and most helpful response. If the bureaucracy which controls the street cleaning services is not responsive, the resident with a dirty street must understand which of the elected officials is most directly responsible for that section of the city in order to obtain better street cleaning. City employees, while generally hardworking and concerned, may go the extra mile if a city council member makes a special request for a constituent. Of course, providing service to constituents can sometimes lead to unethical "favors" for constituents. If

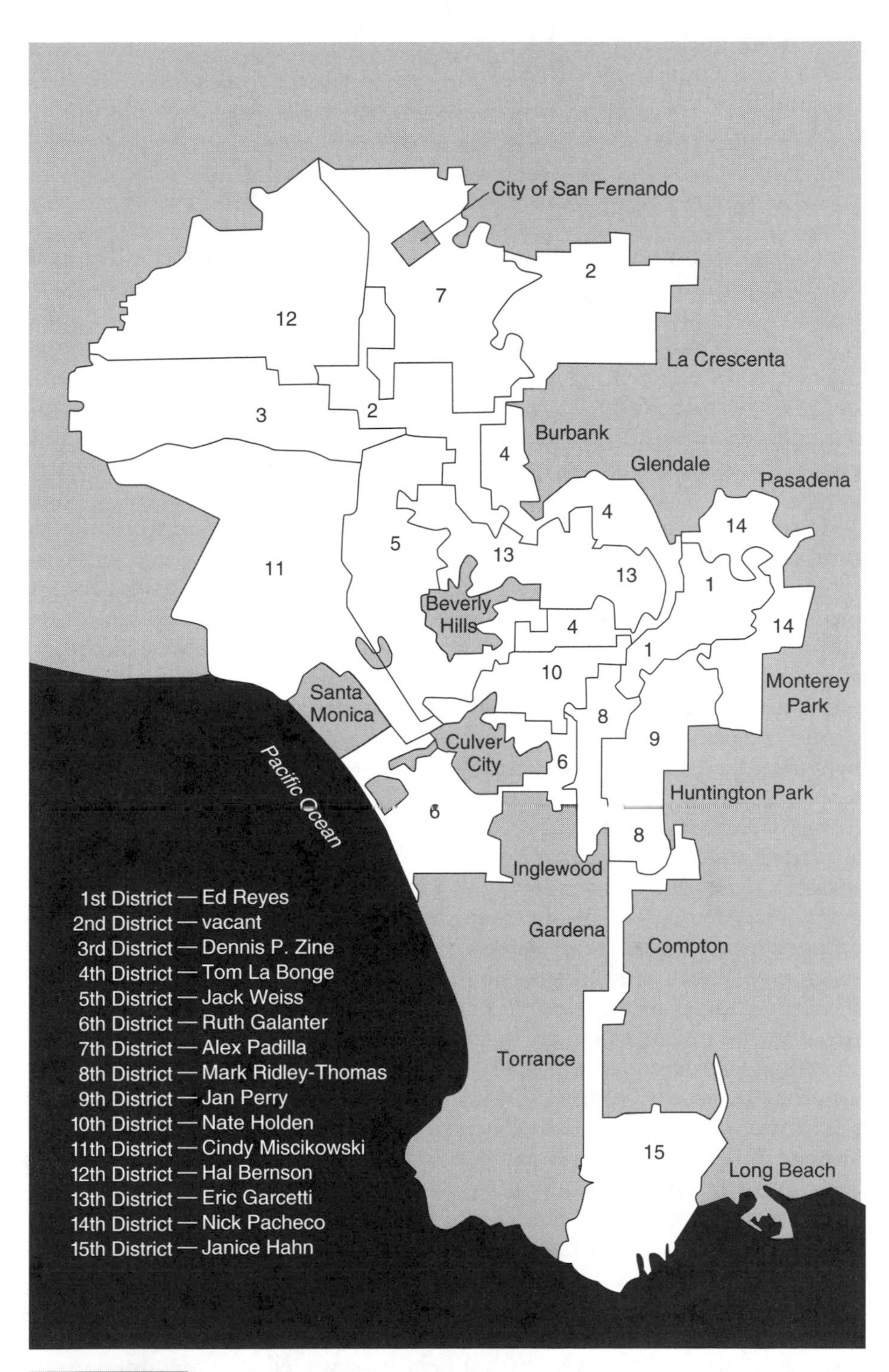

FIGURE 12.1 Los Angeles City Council Districts, 1995.

Source: City Clerk, Los Angeles.

constituents ask for special consideration, such as permission to build larger buildings than current codes permit, outraged citizens may demand investigations of elected officials who try to gain political support through this abuse of power.[3]

City Politics: Power Blocs in Competition

The forces that influence city politics are even more varied than the forms of city government. Homeowners, builders, city employee unions, historic preservationists, environmentalists, realtors, street vendors, renters, and landlords are among the groups which vie for clout in the city's decision-making process. In city elections, as in most political campaigns, incumbents tend to have the advantage, but an incumbent who has made enough enemies can be ousted by a well-organized challenger. In some cities, term limits have been enacted and opportunities for newcomers have increased. Ironically, despite the many issues determined by city councils, some cities have canceled elections due to incumbents running with no opposition.[4]

One of the factors in city politics is whether council members are elected *at-large* or *district-based*. In most of California's nearly 500 cities, council members are elected *at-large*, that is, they may live anywhere in the city. Only a few cities use *district-based* elections, which divide the city into geographic areas from which council members are elected. For years, the argument for at-large elections was that the most qualified people could get into office regardless of their address. However, this often results in large sections of cities, particularly those inhabited by ethnic minorities, not being represented on the council due to the financial advantages of whites from other areas who run for office. In 2000, the U.S. Justice Department sued the city of Santa Paula, alleging that its at-large system has prevented Latinos from getting elected.[5] Those who oppose by-district elections express concerns that districts would lead to *gerrymanders*. Whether under pressure from the federal government or from local residents, most cities that change from at-large to district elections usually experience an increase in ethnic diversity on their councils.

Another factor in how well a council represents city residents is whether the council job is full or part time. In most cities, serving on the city council is a form of community volunteerism, with a small stipend paid for countless hours of city-related tasks. In these cases, those able to run and serve as council members tend to be affluent business people or retired persons. In the few cities, such as Los Angeles, that offer a full-time job to council members, the diversity of professions and backgrounds on the council tends to increase.

In between the four-year election cycle, council business is often handled without much public debate or attention. The battle for power which goes on between elections is most likely to be waged at city council meetings, council committee hearings, or planning commission hearings. At these, residents affected by a potential ordinance are empowered to speak to the issues before the decision-making body. The Brown Act, or "open meeting law," requires that all local government meetings be open to the public except when personnel matters, legal actions, labor negotiations, or property deals are being discussed. Public notice of meetings and their agendas must be made available in advance, although these notices are often tucked away in little-read newspapers. In some cities, cable television offers residents a chance to see their city council in action.

As in all levels of government, city policies are often determined by those who are most able to contribute to campaigns. It is at the city level, however, that well-organized nonaffluent groups can get involved most successfully. Despite fierce opposition from the business community and the mayor, the Los Angeles City Council was sufficiently influenced by a coalition of city workers and antipoverty advocates to pass a veto-proof Living Wage Act in 1997 which mandates that all organizations with city contracts pay their employees a "living" wage higher than the current minimum wage.[6]

Battles over land use and open space are often fought at the city level as developers run into well-organized opposition from environmentalists, homeowners, and public agencies who believe that more buildings will bring increased demands on public services as well as further deterioration of the natural environment. Those who want to build more must increasingly spend large sums for the legal and political battles that surround most major development proposals. A landmark court ruling blocking construction of the 22,000-home Newhall Ranch project due to lack of guaranteed water supplies has reinforced the fact that development in California must take into account the state's natural limitations.[7]

Although many Californians take their city services for granted, the quality of city functions is really determined by the quality of the elected officials and civil servants of any particular city. Disparities in the quality of these services are part of the reason for the vast differentials in property values around our state. A desirable home is a home in a well-run city, and a well-run city is usually one with large numbers of active community members who demand that public officials be accountable to the people.

Questions to Consider

Using Your Text and Your Own Experiences

1. What are the responsibilities of city government? What tax resources can city officials use to accomplish their goals?
2. Compare and contrast the two forms of city government. Which does your city use? What are the pros and cons of each?
3. Discuss the pros and cons of at-large vs. district-based city elections. Which does your city use? Which do you think is best?

Notes

1. Frank Messina, "Drives Toward Cityhood Slowed by Revenue Law," *Los Angeles Times,* 15 July 1997, p. A13.
2. Ed Goldman, "Out of the Sandbox: Sacramento City Politics May Go Bigtime," *California Journal,* May 1993, p. 17.
3. Will Rogers, "Intimidation of City Staff is Rampant, Pair Says," *Glendale NewsPress,* 16 July 1997, p. A1.
4. Douglas P. Shuit, "Lack of Interest Cancels Some Local Elections," *Los Angeles Times,* 21 February 1999, p. A1.
5. Margaret Talev, "U.S. Sues Santa Paula over Voting System," *Los Angeles Times,* 7 April 2000, p. B3.
6. Maryann Mason, "The Living Wage: In the Public Interest?," Chicago Institute on Urban Poverty Paper, 1996.
7. James Flanigan, "Decision Forces New Water Era upon California," *Los Angeles Times,* 7 June 2000, p. C1.

CHAPTER 13

Counties, Special Districts, and Regional Agencies

"Local government offers a unique opportunity for grass-roots politics because it's a setting where big-money interests can't throw around as much weight."

Congressman Bernie Sanders, former mayor of Burlington, VT

Of all governmental units, those at the local level are closest to the people and affect them most personally, through such services as public safety, traffic regulation, and the operation of public schools. One might hope, therefore, that they would be the easiest to understand and control. However, because of the large numbers of local governments and their confusing and overlapping jurisdictions, this is not the case. California has a hodge-podge of over 7,000 local governments with a total of more than 15,000 local elected officials, who often work to provide services duplicated by an agency a few miles away.[1] It is this chaotic approach to local governance that allows for much "local control," but much confusion and overlapping as well.

Counties: Misunderstood but Vital Entities

California's fifty-eight counties are administrative subdivisions of the state and run the gamut in both geographic size and population. Los Angeles County, with close to 9 million residents, is the most populous in the nation. San Bernardino County, with its 20,000 square miles, is the largest in area. In contrast, mountainous Alpine County, which borders Nevada near Lake Tahoe, has about 1,300 residents, and San Francisco, the only combined city-county in the state, comprises only 49 square miles.

For residents of *unincorporated areas*, counties provide the basic "urban" services: safety, road repair, zoning, libraries, and parks. Counties also dispense another complete set of services to all residents, both those in cities and those in unincorporated regions. These programs include administration of welfare programs such as Temporary Assistance to Needy Families (TANF); supervision of foster care and adoptions of abused or neglected children; the maintenance of property ownership, voter registration, and birth and marriage records; the prosecution of felonies; the operation of the Superior Court system; the provision of health services (including mental health) to the uninsured; and control of public health problems such as highly contagious diseases and outbreaks of food poisoning.

In order to provide these varied services, counties must receive financial support from the state and federal governments. Nationwide welfare programs such as TANF receive substantial funds from the federal government, while the state provides a large measure of funding for the county's health care programs and the public protection agencies such as courts, district attorney's office, and county jail. Like the cities, counties have become heavily dependent on Sacramento since Prop. 13. During the lean recession years, counties suffered major cutbacks. Since the state's economic recovery, counties are gradually rebuilding their ability to provide essential services. Nonetheless, continuing needs for financial assistance from the federal and state governments still hampers county officials' independence.

Another serious problem facing California's counties is the overlap of services when cities and counties provide identical services in virtually the same community. County sheriffs' departments continue to serve unincorporated areas just blocks from where those same services are provided by city police departments. In some cases, cities simply shut down their own police or fire departments and ask the county to take over that function for a fee. In other situations, both counties and cities have considered *privatization* of services, a way of contracting with corporations to employ staff without making them government employees. This often involves lower pay and reduced benefits for workers who provide public services. Privatization tends to create strong opposition from public employee organizations and interest groups concerned about the quality of government.

A final problem for counties is the issue of adequate representation. With the exception of San Francisco, with its combined city-county status and its eleven-member board of supervisors, all counties are governed by five-member boards of supervisors, exercising both legislative and executive powers. In less populated counties, five individuals may be sufficient; in counties such as Los Angeles, five supervisors serving 9 million residents clearly seems insufficient. Despite several efforts to increase the size of the Los Angeles County Board of Supervisors, voters have repeatedly rejected such proposals, primarily fearing greater costs. In addition to electing their supervisors, county voters also usually elect a sheriff, district attorney, and tax assessor.

Special Districts: Doing What Only They Can Do

Special districts, most of which were created before Prop. 13 altered the state's financial structure, serve the purpose of providing a specific service that no other jurisdiction provides. Special district services include water supplies, street lighting, mosquito abatement, transportation, and air quality control. With over 5,000 special districts (see Table 13.1), California may take the prize for providing local control of services, but the fiscal consequences are high.[2] Normally, each district performs only one task,

TABLE 13.1

Special District Activities, 1989–1990

Number of Districts	*Activity Category*
1009	K–12 (including K–8 and 9–12)
890	Water utility
783	Lighting and lighting maintenance
586	Fire protection
577	Waste disposal (enterprise)
450	Streets and roads—construction and maintenance
410	Financing and constructing facilities
297	Recreation and park
260	Cemetery
216	Drainage and drainage maintenance
126	Land reclamation and levee maintenance
116	Resource conservation
97	Flood control and water conservation
79	Hospital
72	Community college
71	Ambulance
70	Pest control
55	Waste disposal (nonenterprise)
53	Transit
49	Police protection
48	Electric
47	Local and regional planning or development
41	Government services
37	Library services
34	Air pollution control
27	Memorial
17	Airport
13	Harbor and port
13	Television translator station facilities
11	Parking
8	Health
4	Animal control
6,566	

Source: State Controller's 1989–90 Annual Report.

yet may have a well-paid staff with travel budgets and "perks." Most special districts are governed by the county board of supervisors or their appointees, while some special district boards are elected by the public.

Special districts range in size from small cemetery districts to the Metropolitan Water District of Southern California, which serves six counties and wields enormous political clout, especially during drought periods, when the politics of water distribution become most tense. Other large special districts include the Los Angeles County Metropolitan Transit Authority and the Bay Area Rapid Transit District. The many special districts, both large and small, create both confusion and costs for Californians. In response to complaints about expensive bureaucracies, the Constitutional Revision Commission has suggested a massive overhaul of special districts,[3] but as yet, no such changes have been implemented.

School Districts: The Most Common Special Districts

Of all the services provided by local governments, the biggest and most expensive is public education. This is the responsibility of more than 1,100 special districts, including approximately 630 elementary school districts, 115 high school districts, 72 community college districts, and 285 unified districts providing both elementary and high school programs. These districts each have elected boards whose members are accountable directly to the voters. Their chief revenue source is the state, with some monies still derived from local property taxes.

California's schools were among the best in the nation until Prop. 13 drastically cut the primary funding source. (See Figure 13.1.) For twenty years, the public schools declined in measures such as pupil–teacher ratio, maintenance of school facilities, and number of computers per student. Finally, due to improved tax revenues and public dissatisfaction, politicians finally invested in public schools by mandating smaller classes for all primary grades (K–3). However, local school boards often have had difficulty implementing class size reduction due to lack of space and a shortage of trained teachers. Compounding the overall issue about adequate state funding is the enormous differences in quality between affluent, suburban school districts (where property tax revenues are higher) and the schools in most inner cities.

Along with the thousand or so K–12 special districts, seventy-two community college districts serve the state's adult population. These two-year colleges enable over 1.4 million Californians to earn credits for university transfer, receive vocational training, participate in community volunteerism, or learn English as a Second Language and other basic skills. There are no entrance requirements other than being eighteen years of age (or, in some cases, being approved to attend at a younger age). Those who are California residents pay the lowest fees in the nation, while students from other nations and states pay tuition which is still considerably less than that of most private colleges. California's community colleges offer

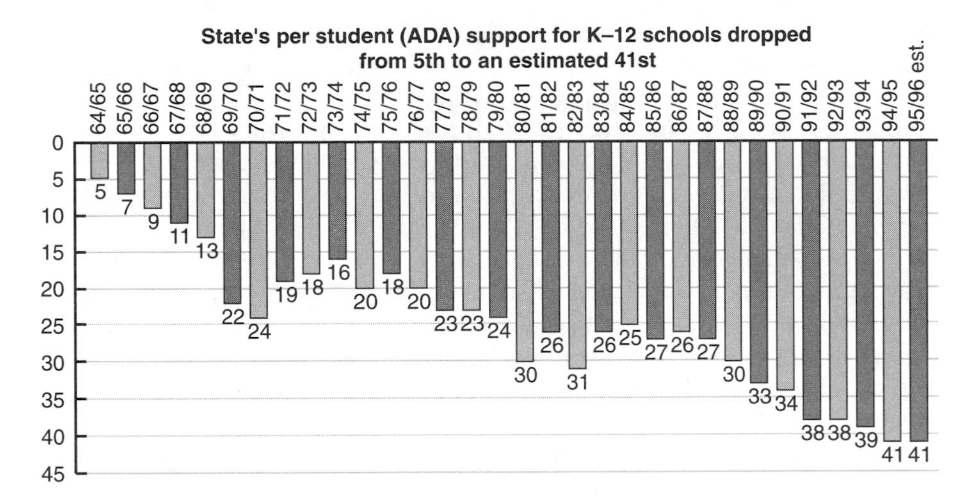

FIGURE 13.1 **California Expenditure per Pupil, Ranking over Time.**
Source: California Department of Education.

an educational bargain for those willing to take advantage of it. Each community college district is managed by a locally elected board of trustees and overseen by a state-level board of governors.

Regional Agencies: Two Types, Two Different Functions

As the problems facing California grow increasingly regional in nature, proposals to enhance the powers of regional agencies abound; yet most regional coordination agencies remain limited in their authority. These agencies have traditionally handled complex issues such air quality, jobs–housing balance, water supplies, and other matters which transcend city and county boundaries. *Multi-issue* regional agencies try to coordinate the tasks and plans of all the various local government units in a region. The five largest intergovernmental "councils of government" are the Association of Bay Area Governments (ABAG), including nine counties and 100 cities in the San Francisco area; the Southern California Association of Governments (SCAG), which embraces six counties and 180 cities; the Sacramento Area Council of Governments (SACOG), including four counties and part of a fifth; the Association of Monterey Bay Area Governments (AMBAG), representing three counties and twenty cities; and the San Diego Association of Governments (SANDAG), including all eighteen cities and the county itself. Historically, these agencies have had no authority to enforce their recommendations, so their "advisory" role has often been ignored by the cities and counties they represent.

Perhaps because of the minimal powers of the multi-issue regional agencies, *single-issue* regional agencies, or large special districts, have developed. Air Quality Management Districts with substantial regulatory powers have been established for Southern California, the San Joaquin Valley, and the San Francisco Bay Area, while water supplies for the southern half of the state are handled through the Metropolitan Water District. Transportation in the Bay Area is handled through the Bay Area Rapid Transit District (BART), while the Los Angeles area is served by the Metropolitan Transit District (MTA). Unfortunately, some of these agencies have been plagued with legal and political problems that keep them from performing their duties efficiently, and public concerns with air and water pollution, traffic congestion, and lack of affordable housing are far from being solved. These problems rarely respect city or county boundaries, yet the current mood of politicians seems to oppose regional problem solving.[4] Perhaps only a regional disaster will bring about the coordination and interdependence that Californians prefer to avoid as they pursue their belief in small government. Like other Americans, Californians value local autonomy and resist empowering larger units of government until insurmountable problems demand it.

Questions to Consider

Using Your Text and Your Own Experiences

1. Describe the responsibilities of counties and their funding base. What are the financial challenges facing California counties?
2. Define special districts and give several examples. Does California need to revise its approach to providing services through special districts? Explain your answer.
3. Why do regional agencies exist? What dilemma do they encounter as they attempt to create regional solutions to problems?

Notes

1. California Constitution Revision Commission, *Final Report and Recommendations to the Governor and Legislature*, Sacramento, 1996, p. 72.
2. "Government in California: Buckling Under the Strain," *The Economist*, 13 February 1993, p. 21.
3. California Constitution Revision Commission, p. 74.
4. Sherry Bebitch Jeffe, "Southern Exposure: The Decline of Regionalism," *California Journal*, August 1997, p. 11.

CHAPTER 14
Financing the Golden State

"... key aspects of the way California collects and apportions tax revenues are greatly flawed. ... The big losers in California's game of fiscal roulette have been its communities and its people."
Antonio Villaraigosa, Speaker Emeritus of the Assembly[1]

Perhaps the most persistent problem of all governments is finding adequate financial resources to do the many tasks expected of the public sector. Even as people complain incessantly about insufficient levels of service, many of them also fiercely resist being taxed to pay for needed improvements. Such contradictions become even more acute in difficult economic times when unemployment rises (thus reducing the total amount of income tax paid) and the needs for unemployment funds or welfare programs increase. In prosperous periods, tax collections generally rise, and politicians are tempted to offer "tax cuts" even though all public services are not fully funded. Whether the economy is booming or in a slump, there are only a few options for government: raise somebody's taxes, provide fewer services, or borrow money and pay it back (with interest, of course) in the future. Each of these has its own consequences and costs, and it is the process of making these decisions that becomes the annual state budget battle.

How the Budget Is Developed: A Two-Year Process

Every January, the governor must present to the legislature a budget plan reflecting the governor's priorities. This budget requires many months of preparation and input from the executive branch's various departments and agencies, under the supervision of the Department of Finance. The budget is based on "guesstimates" of the amount the state will collect in taxes and *"baseline" budgets* from each of the state agencies, cities, counties, and special districts which rely on the state as their primary source of funds. Baseline (or "rollover") budgets essentially assume that an agency needs to continue doing everything it currently does as well as receive some cost-of-living adjustment (COLA) raise from the previous year's budget. Of course, agencies may also ask for new funds to provide additional programs, and the governor may wish to initiate new services or reorganize existing programs.

The governor's budget then is examined by the Legislative Analyst, who reviews the governor's expenditure requests and revenue projections and provides each legislator with comments. Then the legislature begins public hearings held before five subcommittees in each house. During these hearings, government employees at all levels (and their lobbyists) explain why their particular *appropriations* must be maintained or perhaps expanded. Lobbyists for business interests also register their concerns about any tax increases which may negatively affect their industries or attempt to support tax cuts which reduce their costs.

It is during these budget hearings that the day dreaded by many Californians arrives: April 15. Once tax day is over, the Director of Finance knows more clearly how much the state has received in personal income taxes and can reevaluate earlier revenue projections to determine whether or not the original budget is accurate. Based on these revised numbers, the governor submits to the legislature the "May revise." If the Assembly and Senate disagree on specific items, a conference committee must be formed to work out the differences.

The final budget agreement is supposed to be complete by June 15 and signed by the governor by June 30. (See Table 14.1.) Prior to the Davis administration, this process was rarely completed on time. However, Governor Davis has insisted on receiving the budget and making his final veto decisions by deadline, a goal facilitated by having Democrats hold the majority in both houses. In recent years, the minor delays in completing the budget were generally due to a small number of Republicans whose votes were essential for the required two-thirds majority but whose budget priorities differed from those of the Democratic majority.

Once the budget bill reaches the governor, the chief executive can then utilize the *item veto* to reduce appropriations or even eliminate whole programs. The legislature rarely has the two-thirds majority to override specific item vetoes, leaving the governor in ultimate control over state spending.

Sources of Revenue: Never Enough

The five major sources of money for the state are:

1. The general fund, which includes state income tax, sales taxes, bank and corporations taxes, and interest earned by the state on money not currently in use
2. Special funds, including motor vehicle license and registration fees, gasoline taxes, and portions of the sales, cigarette, and horse racing taxes which are earmarked for specified purposes

TABLE 14.1

California Budget Process

Executive Branch		*Legislative Branch*
Administrative departments prepare budgetary requests.	April	
Agencies prepare preliminary program budgets.	May	
Department of Finance and governor issue policy directions.	July August	
Department of Finance reviews agency proposals.	September October	
Commission on State Finance and experts forecast revenues.	November	
Governor finalizes budget and sends it to the state printing office.	January	
January 10: Governor submits budget to legislature.		Fiscal committee chairs introduce governor's proposal as budget bill.
	February	Legislative analyst studies proposed budget; issues *Analysis of Budget Bill* and *Perspectives and Issues.*
	March	
	April	Assembly and Senate budget subcommittees hold public hearings on assigned sections of the budget.
Department of Finance issues revised forecast of revenues and expenditures.	May	Subcommittees complete action on budget.
		Full budget committees hold hearings and vote.
		Assembly and Senate pass respective versions of the budget bill.
	June	Conference committee of 3 Assembly members and 3 senators agree on a compromise budget bill.
		June 15: Legislature submits approved budget to governor.
June 30: Governor exercises item veto and signs budget act.	July	Legislature can restore vetoed items by two-thirds vote in each house.

3. Bond funds, requiring voter approval, which are monies borrowed from investors and returned to them with interest in the future
4. Federal funds, including "free" money and some grants which require matching state or local commitments
5. Miscellaneous revenues, such as community college fees, contributions to state pension plans, etc.

Figures 14.1 and 14.2 show state revenues and expenditures.

Controversies over these revenue sources are endless. Which taxes should be raised? Which lowered? Business interests want to reduce any taxes which cut into their profits, while individuals almost always seem to feel that they are paying "too much tax." The Republican viewpoint has traditionally insisted on reducing taxes regardless of impacts on programs, while Democrats have often proposed closing loopholes that benefit the wealthy in order to protect low-income residents. Voters must decide whether to support *bond issues* and numerous local assessments, and their record suggests that during hard times they tend not to authorize gov-

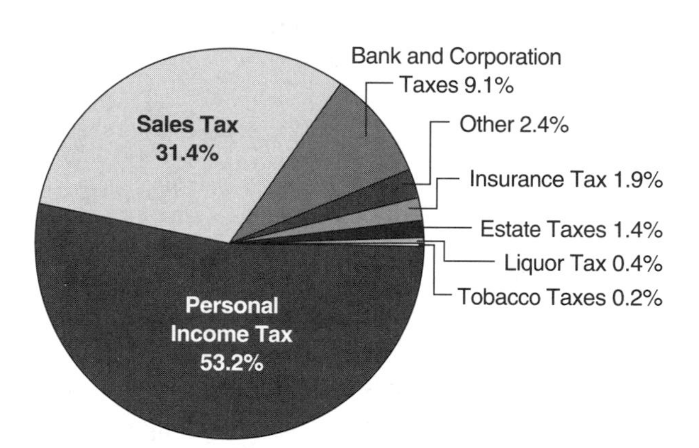

FIGURE 14.1 General Fund Revenues and Transfers, 2000–2001

Source: California Department of Finance

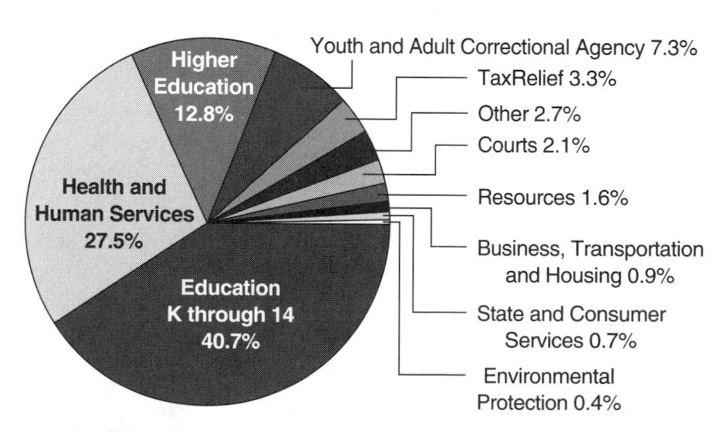

FIGURE 14.2 General Fund Expenditures, 2000–2001

Source: California Department of Finance

ernment spending or borrowing, but that during improved economic periods they are more willing to vote for school bonds and other public expenditures. While state bonds pass with a simple majority, local bonds for decades required a two-thirds majority, which prevented numerous school bonds from passing. This requirement was finally reduced to 55 percent when Prop. 39 (2000) was approved. The 55 percent majority for local school and college bonds is expected to reinvigorate public education as districts promote and pass measures authorizing new school construction.

Voter Decisions and State Finance: Democracy in Action?

In addition to voting on bond measures, voters have utilized ballot initiatives to make fiscal policy for the state. One of the turning points for California's tax policies was Prop. 13 of June 1978, also known as the Jarvis-Gann initiative in recognition of the efforts of landlord Howard Jarvis and his ally Paul Gann to get the initiative on the ballot. Although its passage occurred over two decades ago, Prop. 13's causes and consequences are still vital elements in understanding California's situation today.

The roots of Prop. 13 lay in the massive national and international *inflation* of the early 1970s. While the causes of the inflationary spiral were primarily outside California, including such factors as heavy federal spending in the 1960s and the oil embargo of the early 1970s, these circumstances, added to the traditional speculation in land and property in the state, fueled an enormous rise in the real estate values on which property taxes are levied. People who had lived in homes for years were suddenly confronted with doubled and tripled *tax assessments* from their county assessor. Faced with the risk of losing their homes, middle–and low-income homeowners gladly joined Jarvis and other major property holders in supporting Prop. 13. When public employees claimed that the proposition would not only cut property taxes on which local governments relied heavily, but also cut public services, Jarvis replied that "only the fat" would be cut and that the state budget would rescue counties, cities, and school districts if necessary.

These arguments were extremely persuasive—Prop. 13 passed by a landslide, and all property taxes were limited to 1 percent of the assessed value of the property as of 1976, with reassessment to occur only when the property was sold. Since a budget surplus had accumulated in Sacramento, the state did "bail out" the local governments for a while, but many services were cut back, including library accessibility, fine arts and athletics in the schools, and parks and recreation. Additionally, Prop. 13 had some unforeseen long-term impacts, including the shift from local control to a Sacramento-based funding system for most of the cities, counties, and special districts. Other flaws in the measure include the fact that property owners who rarely sell (such as commercial property owners) have almost no increase in taxes, whereas owners of individual homes, which are sold more frequently, confront reassessments up to the current market value, causing dramatic tax increases. Even two neighboring homeowners in identical homes may pay vastly differing property taxes based upon when they purchased their homes. This disparity led the U.S. Supreme Court to refer to Prop. 13 as "distasteful and unwise," even as the Court upheld the legality of the law in a 1991 challenge.

During tight economic times, the state's ability to assist local governments which lost revenues due to Prop. 13 is reduced. More recently, with state coffers full, legislators and the governor have increased state support to some areas of local government. County judicial systems finally became fully state funded just a few years ago, while state resources for K–12 schools have increased. However, cities, counties, and community college districts continue to go on annual "begging" expeditions to Sacramento, and in recent years the combined costs of lobbying Sacramento have made local governments, as a whole, one of the most high-spending lobbying categories.[2]

Through their ballot activism, voters have also placed tight restrictions on the state budget itself. Proposition 98 (1988) requires the state to spend 40 percent of its annual revenue on K–14 education, while another 15–20 percent of the budget is set aside to finance bond commitments and voter-mandated programs such as prison construction. Another 25–30 percent of the budget is mandated by federal law to provide health and welfare assistance, although federal welfare reform does permit the state somewhat more flexibility in how it provides "temporary aid to needy families" (TANF). Ultimately, the annual budget battle is really a debate about the remaining 15–20 percent of the budget pie.[3]

Future Prospects: The Permanent Debate

California and its people suffered greatly during the economic downturn of the early 1990s. Massive job losses in aerospace and defense combined with downsizing and mergers in banking and other industries to create lowered tax revenues. Meanwhile, the newly unemployed needed state programs to retrain as well as income support during difficult times. Reduced revenues and increased demands for government services always create a tense political struggle over state budget priorities.

However, since the economic rebound, many Californians are seeing their personal income increase, and those fortunate enough to own property have seen their values skyrocket. Economists predict continued strong growth in entertainment, tourism, trade, agriculture, textiles, and high-tech. But no matter how well some individuals may do, economic growth does not create comfort for all. The state must offer high-quality education at all levels to all its residents, and it must imprison convicted criminals and assist the needy. Even in prosperous times, California still has numerous residents who remain unemployed, undereducated, and/or in poor health. Because of all the demands, state budget battles continue whether the economy is in boom or bust.

Each year as the budget cycle proceeds, hundreds of unique groups demand government support, including school children and their parents, open-space advocates, prison guards, public employees, library users, college students, welfare (TANF) recipients, automobile users, beachgoers, legal immigrants, disabled, farm workers, landowners—the list is endless. For the foreseeable future, California's budget process is bound to be an annual agony that profoundly affects all Californians, yet is carried out in Sacramento conference rooms far from the scrutiny of television news cameras. Until more Californians pay attention to this process, and communicate their preferences to their elected officials, the voices and views of the majority may not be reflected in the budget outcome.

Questions to Consider

Using Your Text and Your Own Experiences

1. How does the general economy affect government budgets? What is the role of government in helping the economy grow?
2. Describe the revenue sources and expense patterns of state government. Who benefits from the current structure? Who loses?
3. Evaluate the budget process through its annual cycle. What are some problems with the process? Should anything be changed?

Notes

1. Honorable Antonio R. Villaraigosa, "A Message from the Speaker," Final Report of the Speaker's Commission on State and Local Government Finance, March 2000, p. 3.
2. Secretary of State, *Lobbying Expenditures and the Top 100 Lobbying Firms,* April 1–June 30, 1994, issued September 1994.
3. "Government in California: Buckling Under the Strain," *The Economist,* 13 February 1993, pp. 21–23.

CHAPTER 15

Issues for the New Century

"In contemporary California, for democracy to be meaningful it must consider all people residing in the state as potential citizens. A modern democracy cannot survive when there are entire categories of excluded people."

Stephanie S. Pincetl, professor of Environmental Studies[1]

According to polls, Californians celebrated their sesquicentennial and the New Millennium by rediscovering some of their traditional optimism. Despite long-term predictions of severe climate changes due to global warming,[2] the new century began with no major natural disasters. Perhaps the only cloud on California's sunny horizon is the drastic increase in electricity and natural gas costs that apparently resulted from an overzealous *deregulation* law passed in the 1990s. The long-term impacts on consumers and business has not yet been fully analyzed. Meanwhile, in general, the economy is flourishing and bringing rewards to those with the education and drive to take advantage of today's opportunities. Nonetheless, the state has many challenges ahead. While some people are enjoying the material success that has often defined the California dream, others continue to experience the dream as a myth (see Figure 15.1). Will the future be best if politicians cut taxes and services so people rely more on themselves, or if they tax those who have achieved abundance in order to help the "have-nots"? This perennial question, often representing the poles that divide Republicans from Democrats, continues to face voters and politicians who care about the fate of the Golden State.

The Challenges Ahead: Evolving into the New Century

As the world shrinks due to technological change, California continues to be well positioned for the increasingly global marketplace. Positioned next

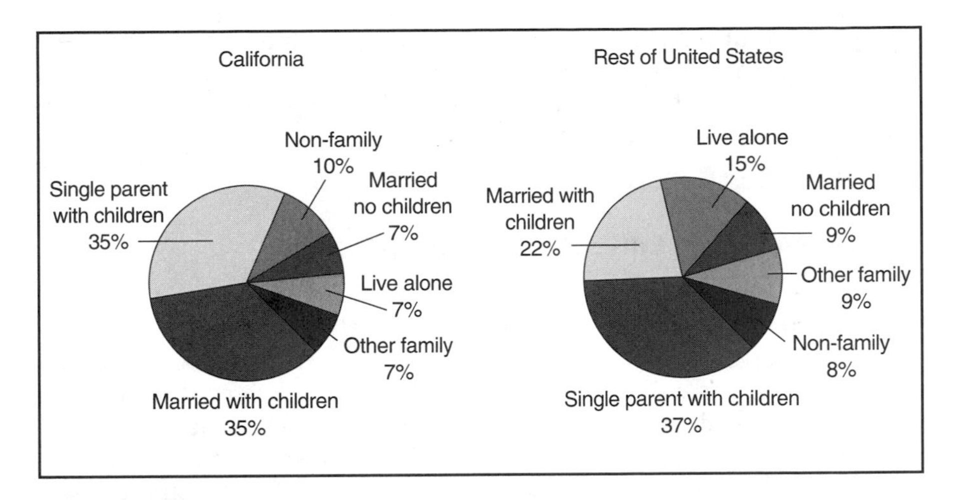

FIGURE 15.1 Distribution of People in Poverty by Household and Family Type, 1997–1998

to Mexico and with busy harbors ready for ships from the Far East, California benefits more than most states from the global economy. Yet the opening of foreign trade through the North American Free Trade Agreement (NAFTA), the General Agreement on Trade and Tariffs (GATT), and new treaties with China has also brought concerns. Should truckers from Mexico cross into California to bring Mexican produce and products when those trucks and drivers are not held to American standards of safety? Should *maquiladoras*, or border factories, be allowed to pay poverty-level *peso* wages for work once done by decently paid American workers? "Free trade" is not necessarily "fair trade," and because of California's easy accessibility to Mexico and the Far East, Californians must continue to monitor the ways in which foreign trade affects their living standards.

Along with a strong base in foreign trade, our economy has boomed in both new and renewed industries such as biomedical manufacturing, entertainment, and software production. However, high-paying jobs available in these industries can be gained only by those with specialized skills and training. Those who hire talent for these booming industries continue to complain that the state's poorly funded K–12 educational system does not produce the kind of skilled workers needed.[3] Despite campaign promises, Governor Davis and fellow Democrats in the legislature have found that educational reforms are slow to take effect, and it may take decades to repair the damages of past political and budgetary decisions. One highly hopeful note for Californians is recent legislation which guarantees vastly expanded financial aid for college-bound students.[4]

Along with the challenges of *globalization* of the economy and educating Californians for the high-tech future, other concerns that must be addressed include the continuing gap between rich and poor; the difficulties created by the cultural diversity that also enriches California life; the conflicts involved in managing a complex ecosystem; and the serious question as to whether or not California is "governable."

Causes and Consequences: Understanding Today's Situation

In recovering from the deep recession of the early 1990s, California business shifted away from reliance on federal military contracts and diversified into many new areas. This *demilitarization* has evolved into an economy that is dependent on technology and private business rather than government-funded military preparations. However, more than ever, the jobs available in the new economy are polarized between well-paying, high-education careers and low-paying, low-skill jobs. In the "middle" of the economy, many blue-collar manufacturing jobs have been relocated to low-wage, nonunion sites, and the white-collar middle class which cannot relocate (teachers, office workers, public employees) is under severe pressure just to find affordable housing.[5] The near disappearance of factory work leaves behind a *service* economy based not on producing goods but on exchanging services, including entertainment, tourism, telecommunications, retail sales, law, financial services, health care, education, software, and so forth. In virtually all of these service industries, only the highly educated can move into the upper levels, while those whose education is inadequate usually labor for minimum wage or even less. This produces a *two-tier economy* that drastically skews the social and political system. Voter turnout is always high among the affluent and low among the less educated and those of lower income. While the upper class votes, the *underclass* often feels powerless and neglects to exercise this right.

Perhaps the lack of political action on the part of the poor can be attributed to their daily struggle to survive. Research indicates that the gap between rich and poor is not because the rich are getting richer and the poor are remaining the same, but because of "a decline in the income of poor individuals and households."[6] In low-income families, children of working parents rarely have medical insurance, leaving one in six California children without medical coverage.[7] Housing is scarcely affordable even to the middle class, and those with low incomes can rarely join the California dream as homeowners.[8] Being poor is difficult, especially in a place where the contrasts with affluence are highly visible. While Silicon Valley's "dot.com" millionaires are increasing rapidly, the area still has nearly 5,000 identified homeless people, of whom 40 percent are families with children.[9]

These vast gaps are somewhat similar to the class structure in nondemocratic and nonindustrial societies (the "Third World"), and the consequences of the continuing income disparity are rarely talked about by political leaders, often because they fear offending those who finance their campaigns.

One contributing factor in this enormous *class gap* is the *regressive* tax system, which taxes the poor a greater share of their income than the rich, in part through subsidizing business and long-time property owners through Prop. 13, then replacing lost property tax revenues with sales taxes, utilities taxes, and other taxes the poor cannot avoid. Even so-called tax cuts supported by recent legislation do not provide much relief for those too poor to file an income tax return.

As the industrial economy declines, to be replaced by new technologically based industries, human adjustments to these changes continue to involve economic and social stress. While new technology brings new opportunities, it also slams the doors on many workers. In the growing service sector, technological developments allow fewer people to provide the same services. Entire occupations are near obsolescence, including bank tellers, grocery checkers, and others whose work can be done by computers. While some services must remain in California to serve their customers, others move portions of their business out of state for the same reasons that manufacturers leave. With increasing avenues of communication, including email, the Internet and fax machines, many businesses can operate in states or even nations where wages are lower and corporate taxes less burdensome while still serving clients inside California. The service sector of the economy, while growing, often provides low-wage jobs such as restaurant servers, hotel maids, and janitors, none of whom earn wages comparable to the skilled blue-collar jobs in steel, tires, and automobile assembly which used to be readily available in California.

During good times, when the majority of Californians feel prosperous and secure, there is less obvious prejudice and *scapegoating*. However, during times of economic downturn or insecurity, fears of competition for economic "goodies" can cause minor prejudices to become full-fledged ethnic rivalries. As more and more Californians are "new neighbors" with different backgrounds and customs, nearly every ethnic group, including the former majority white population, becomes more concerned for its own survival. Demographic data clearly indicates that California's future is multilingual, multicultural, and multiracial. However, due to a variety of historical and social factors, those who currently vote are mostly white, older, and well-to-do. How the gaps between the "old" California and the "new" California will be closed is not yet known. The challenge is to *acculturate* and assimilate new arrivals without destroying their unique cultural identities and without sacrificing the gains of the American-born population. Part of the solution to this challenge is to provide resources for an outstanding educational system which can help people overcome language barriers, cultural stereotypes, and *ethnocentrism* as well as teach the technological skills and critical thinking essential for success in today's competitive world.

Cultural diversity can enrich daily life through the mingling of music, food, art, language, and even love (one-sixth of all children born in California have parents whose ethnic backgrounds are different from each other,)[10] or it can be used to divide communities and individuals. During periods when the economy is growing, the need to blame usually is reduced, and calls to block the borders and shut down the safety net are heard less frequently. However, it is in the hard times, when jobs are scarce and government revenues are reduced, that political leaders must show their skill and compassion by emphasizing social unity rather than divisive politics of blame. That ability to show compassion and emphasize social unity may increase as political leaders from diverse backgrounds enter the halls of leadership. One hopeful sign is the substantial increase in Latino political strength; perhaps that community will set the example for the growing Asian groups. Clearly, all ethnic groups must work toward the common goals of all Californians, rather than emphasize an ugly, divisive approach to solving problems.

Even as Californians struggle to figure out how to live in the most multicultural state, other problems must not be forgotten. The state's ecosystem continues to require attention even during periods when environmental problems are not in the headlines. Debates over the proper management of California's magnificent natural resources involve numerous special-interest groups as well as many concerned individuals. The continuing destruction of agricultural land to meet the housing and shopping needs of a growing population (see Figure 15.2), the unresolved battles over water supplies, the battles over where to dump the inevitable toxic wastes of a chemically dependent economy, and the debates over how to clean California's air and water all contribute to the long list of vital issues that must be faced by elected officials and the public. With little publicity, environmental battles are constantly fought. The skirmishes take place in legislative committees, at community meetings, and at environmentally sensitive sites throughout the state. In addition to those mentioned above, issues include how to clean up the beaches and bays, how much pesticides can be tolerated on our farms and on our food, how ancient forests can be preserved, where virgin land can be developed, and, in general, how to balance the needs of nature with the needs of the over 33 million human beings in the state. Short-term needs for profit and jobs often conflict with long-term needs to preserve irreplaceable natural wonders, and California's large share of nature's spectacular sites suggests that Californians will be struggling to find the right balance for years to come.

Although not every Californian is equally concerned about environmental issues, the longstanding belief that environmentalism is a white, middle-class hobby has been challenged. In fact, it is the underrepresented ethnic groups who often shoulder the burden of environmental damage. Many of the state's toxic waste dumps are located in minority communities, and rates of asthma and other respiratory diseases are worse in inner cities than in suburbs. Latinos lead the state's ethnic groups in their con-

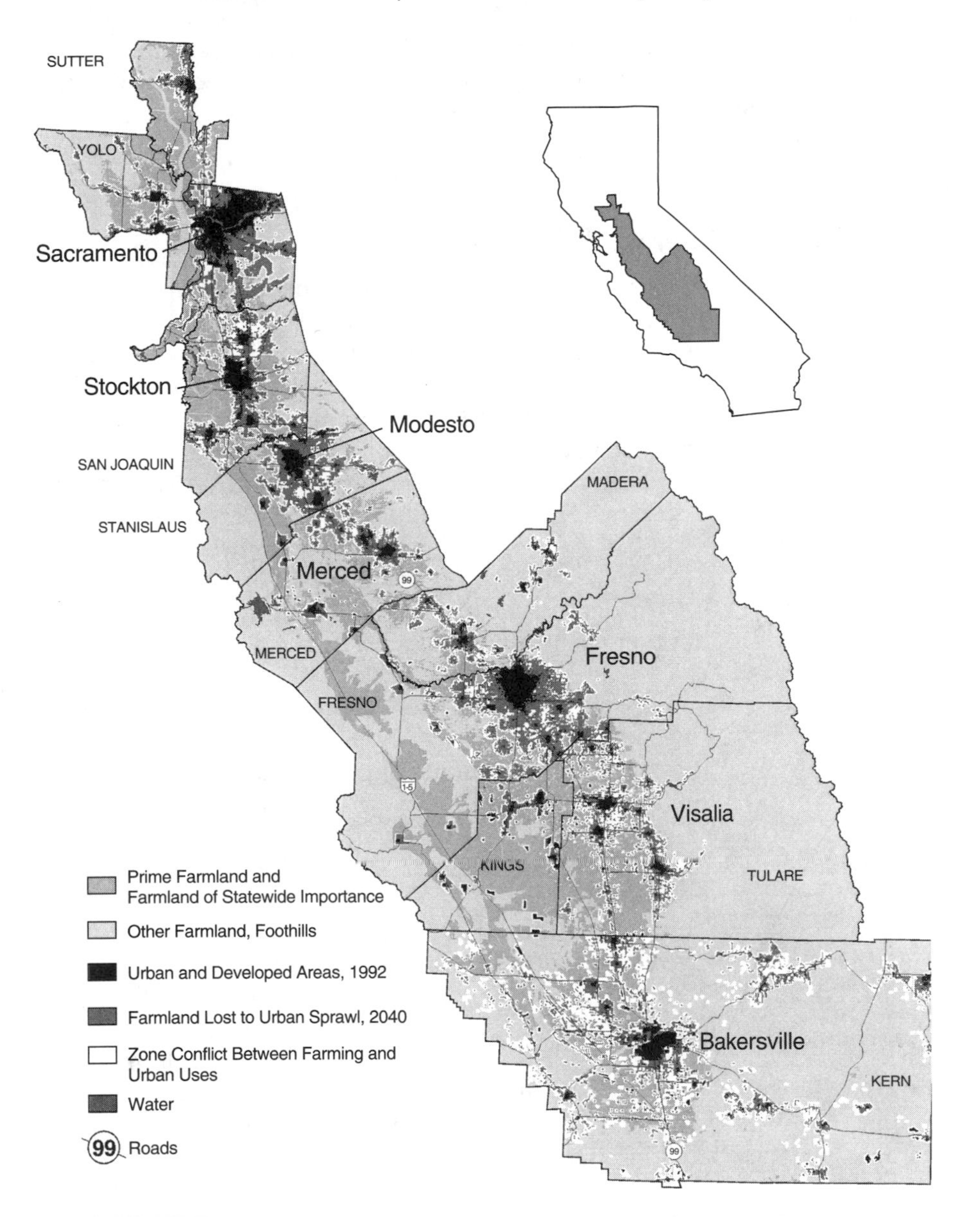

FIGURE 15.2 California's Central Valley: Urban Sprawl by 2040

Source: American Farmland Trust, *Alternatives for Furure Urban Growth in California's Central Valley.*

cern about the environment, with air pollution being the number-one issue for all Californians.[11] While environmental racism is not a common term, it has come to denote the recognition that ethnic minorities often live in the worst ecological circumstances. The growing environmental concerns in communities of color include questions about lead residues in residential housing, water quality in urban areas, and asbestos abatement in public facilities. Once again, these issues can either unite or divide Californians, perhaps depending on how public leaders present them to the people.

Is California Governable?

Facing such enormous challenges, California needs good political leadership more than ever. Decisions about how to respond to national and global economic changes, integrate the increasingly diverse population, provide adequate education and other services to all Californians, regulate business enough to protect people and their environment yet keep corporations from leaving the state, protect irreplaceable natural resources—all of these tasks face a divided state government, which often appears most concerned about its own perks and privileges. Divisions abound: within the parties and between them, between the "oldtimers" and the "newcomers" in government, and among the many special-interest groups which manipulate so much of the decision-making process. To some extent, these conflicts represent inevitable clashes of legitimate yet contradictory perspectives. But the average Californian, trying to earn a living, enjoy a family, and find some security for the future, often appears to have faded from the minds of those in power.

Until each of us recognizes the unique opportunities of the state, and joins with other concerned citizens to right the existing wrongs, it may well be that the Golden State will never again fully reflect the historic "dream." That would be a profound disservice to the Californians of today and those of tomorrow. We can only hope that Californians will pull together to avoid this tragic outcome. Californians of all backgrounds must strive to ensure that all ethnic and cultural groups participate and that all elected officials increase their responsiveness to the public (and perhaps reduce their level of service to narrow special-interest groups). No one group can dominate in a state that no longer has a single majority group. It will be the responsibility of the most educated and concerned members of every group to mobilize their friends and associates to join in active, organized efforts to improve life in California.

Unless the general public understands these challenges and their role in them, the future will never be as golden as the state's historic promise. Everyone, to varying degrees, uses the services provided through our state and local governments: airports, highways, beaches, schools, disability checks, community college classes, libraries, drivers licenses, professional licenses, county hospitals—the list is endless. All of us must remember that these services require public money which must be allocated carefully and spent wisely. Those who protest endlessly about paying their share must remember the part of the American ethic which says "United we stand, divided we fall." No Californian can be an island; each and every one must share the benefits and pay the costs of life in California, the most awesome of states.

Questions to Consider

Using Your Text and Your Own Experiences

1. What are some of the strengths and weaknesses of today's economy? What can state government do to enhance the economic well-being of the state's people? Should government be involved in promoting economic well-being?
2. What are some strengths and weaknesses of California's political and social circumstances? Who benefits and who loses in the current system? How are you affected by this situation?
3. What can you do to make California a better place to live?

Notes

1. Stephanie S. Pincetl, *Transforming California: A Political History of Land Use and Development,* Johns Hopkins University Press, 1999, p. 318.
2. Kenneth R. Weiss, "Harsh Change Predicted for State Climate," *Los Angeles Times,* 13 June 2000, p. A1.
3. Emelyn Rodriguez, "A Stubborn Digital Divide," *California Journal,* July 2000, pp. 18–22.
4. Jill Leovy, "Legislature Set to OK Major Increase in College Aid," *Los Angeles Times,* 24 August 2000, p. A1.
5. William Fulton and Paul Shigley, "Trying to Balance Jobs and Housing," *California Journal,* July 2000, p. 30–35.
6. Deborah Reed, "Income Inequality in California Outpaces U.S.," Public Affairs Report, Public Policy Institute of California, September 1996, p. 3.
7. Julie Marquis, " 'Shocking' Lack Cited in Child Health Insurance," *Los Angeles Times,* 3 March 1977, p. B1.
8. Diane Wedner, "California Home Sales, Prices Post Records in May," *Los Angeles Times,* 27 June 2000, p. C1.
9. Lisa Fernandez, "Down and Out in Silicon Valley," *California Journal,* July 2000, pp. 44–47.
10. Bettina Boxall and Ray F. Herndon, "Far from Urban Gateways, Racial Lines Blur in Suburbs," *Los Angeles Times,* 15 August 2000, p. A1.
11. Nancy Vogel, "Pollution Concerns Latinos More Than Most Residents, Poll Finds," *Los Angeles Times,* 22 June 2000, p. A3.

APPENDIX A

Directory of Political Organizations That Anyone Can Join

American Independent Party (conservative minor party)
1084 W. Marshall Blvd.
San Bernardino, CA 92405
www.aipca.org

Anti-Defamation League (antidiscrimination, antibigotry)
7851 Mission Center Court #320
San Diego, CA 92108
www.adl.org

Asian Pacific American Legal Center (civil rights issues)
5 Wilshire Blvd.
Los Angeles, CA 90017
www.apanet.org

California Abortion Rights Action League (pro-choice)
8455 Beverly Blvd. Suite 303
Los Angeles, CA 90048
www.choice.org

California Coalition for Investor Responsibility (investing public pension funds responsibly)
1215 K Street, Suite 1920
Sacramento, CA 95814

California Public Interest Research Group (CALPIRG) (consumer and environmental issues)
3435 Wilshire #308
Los Angeles, CA 90010
www.pirg.org/calpirg

California Rural Legal Assistance Fund (legal help in rural areas)
2115 Kern St.
Fresno, CA 93721
www.crla.org

California Tomorrow (making diversity work/children's issues)
436 14th St.
Oakland, CA 94612
www.californiatomorrow.org

California Voter Foundation (using the Web to be informed)
2401 L St.
Sacramento, CA 95816
www.calvoter.org

Children Now—California (children's health, education, etc.)
1212 Broadway, 5th floor
Oakland, CA 94612
www.childrennow.org

Coalition Against Police Abuse (police behavior issues)
2824 S. Western Ave.
Los Angeles, CA 90018

Coalition for Clean Air (air quality issues)
10780 Santa Monica Blvd.
Los Angeles, CA 90025
www.coalitionforcleanair.org

Coalition for Economic Survival (tenants' rights)
1296 N. Fairfax Ave.
West Hollywood, CA 90046

Common Cause (quality of government issues)
926 J St.
Sacramento, CA 95814
www.commoncause.org

Democratic Party of California (partisan)
911 20th St.
Sacramento, CA 95814
www.ca-dem.org

Gay and Lesbian Alliance Against Defamation (monitoring homophobia in media)
8455 Beverly Blvd. #305
Los Angeles, CA 90048
www.glaad.org

Green Party (environmental justice/nonviolence)
1008 10th St. #482
Sacramento, CA 95814
www.greens.org/california

Handgun Control Inc. (gun control lobby)
703 Market Street #1511
San Francisco, CA 94103
www.handguncontrol.org

Health Access (affordable health care for Californians)
942 Market St. #402
San Francisco, CA 94102

JERICHO: A Voice for Justice (social justice issues)
926 J Street
Sacramento, CA 95814

Japanese American Citizens League (civil rights)
1765 Sutter St.
San Francisco, CA 94115
www.jacl.org

Labor/Community Strategy Center (environmental/social justice)
3780 Wilshire Blvd., Suite 1200
Los Angeles, CA 90010
www.thestrategycenter.org

League of Conservation Voters—California (environmental)
1212 Broadway, Suite 630
Oakland, CA 94612
www.lcv.org

League of Women Voters of California (nonpartisan political reform issues)
926 J Street #515
Sacramento, CA 95814
www.smartvoter.org

Libertarian Party of California (antigovernment minor party)
655 Lewelling Blvd., Suite 362
San Leandro, CA 94579
www.lp.org

Liveable Wage Coalition (reducing poverty)
660 Sacramento St. #202
San Francisco, CA 94111

Mexican American Legal Defense and Education Foundation (civil rights)
660 Market St.
San Francisco, CA 94194
www.maldef.org

National Association for the Advancement of Colored People (one of the first civil rights groups)
3910 W. Martin Luther King, Jr. Blvd.
Los Angeles, CA 90008
www.naacp.org

National Conference for Community and Justice (diversity training, human relations)
3258 Fourth Ave.
San Diego, CA 92103
www.nccj.org

National Organization for Women (women's issues)
926 J Street #523
Sacramento, CA 95814
www.now.org

Natural Law Party (meditation as political action)
P.O. Box 50843
Palo Alto, CA 94303
www.natural-law.org/California.html

Planned Parenthood of California (family planning lobby)
2415 K St.
Sacramento, CA 95816
www.plannedparenthood.org

Planning and Conservation League (environmental issues)
926 J St.
Sacramento, CA 95814
www.pcl.org

Republican Party of California (partisan)
1903 W. Magnolia Blvd.
Burbank, CA 91505
www.cagop.org

Sierra Club (environmental issues)
2530 San Pablo Ave.
Berkeley, CA 94702
www.sierraclub.org

Southern California Library for Social Studies and Research (social movement documents/conferences)
6120 S. Vermont Ave.
Los Angeles, CA 90044
www.socallib.org

Southwest Voter Research/William C. Velasquez Institute (encourage Latino voting and political action)
2914 N. Main St., 2nd floor
Los Angeles, CA 90031
800-222-5654
www.svrep.org

Traditional Values Group (conservative Christian lobby)
1127 11th St.
Sacramento, CA 95814
www.traditionalvalues.org

The Utility Reform Network (TURN) (consumer advocacy)
711 Van Ness, Suite 350
San Francisco, CA 94105
www.turn.org

United Students Against Sweatshops (globalization issues)
310 8th Street
Oakland, CA 94607
www.sweatshopwatch.org

APPENDIX B

California State Offices

Constitutional Officers

(All area codes 916 unless otherwise noted)

Governor's Office

Gray Davis (D)
Elected: 1998
Term Limit: 2006
http://www.governor.ca.gov/state/govsite/gov homepage.jsp
1st Floor State Capitol
Sacramento 95814
445–2841
Fax: 445–4633

300 S Spring St #16701
Los Angeles 90013
(213) 897–0322
Fax: (213) 897–0319

455 Golden Gate Ave #14000
San Francisco 94102
(415) 703–2218
Fax: (415) 703–2803

1350 Front St 6054
San Diego 92101
(619) 525–4641
Fax: (619) 525–4640

2550 Mariposa Mall #3013
Fresno 93721
(559) 445–5295
Fax: (559) 445–5328

3737 Main St #201
Riverside 92501
(909) 680–6860
Fax: (909) 680–6863

444 N Capitol St NW
Washington, DC 20001
(202) 624–5270
Fax: (202) 624–5280

Cabinet

Lynn Schenk, COS
445–2841

Susan Kennedy, Dpty COS Cabinet Affairs
445–6131

Tim Gage, Dir of Department of Finance
445–3878

William J. Lyons, Secy of Department of Food and Agriculture
654–0433

Stephen J. Smith, Dir of Department of Industrial Relations
(415) 703–5050

Bruce Thiesen, Interim Secy of Department of Veterans Affairs
653–2535

Maria Contreras-Sweet, Agency Secy of Business, Transportation and Housing Agency
323–5400

Winston H. Hickox, Agency Secy of California Environmental Protection Agency
445–3846

Kerry Mazzoni, Secy for Education
323–0611

Grantland Johnson, Agency Secy of Health and Human Services Agency
654–3454

Mary Nichols, Secy for Resources of Resources Agency
653–5656

Aileen Adams, Agency Secy of State and Consumer Services Agency
653–2636

Lon S. Hatamiya, Agency Secy of Technology, Trade and Commerce Agency
322–1394

Robert Presley, Secy of Youth and Adult Correctional Agency
323–6001

Special Offices

Department of Finance
Dir: Tim Gage
http://www.dof.ca.gov
1145 Capitol Building
Sacramento 95814
445–3878
Fax: 324–7311

Department of Food and Agriculture
Secy: William J. Lyons
http://www.cdfa.ca.gov
1220 N St #409
Sacramento 95814
654–0433
Fax: 654–0403

Department of Industrial Relations
Dir: Stephen J. Smith
http://www.dir.ca.gov
Box 420603
San Francisco 94142
(415) 703–5050
Fax: (415) 703–5059

Department of Veterans Affairs
Interim Secy: Bruce Thiesen
http://www.ns.net/cadva
1227 O St
Sacramento 95814
653–2535
Fax: 653–1960

Office of Administrative Law
Dir: Vacant
Dpty Dir/Chf Cnsl: David B. Judson
http://www.oal.ca.gov
555 Capitol Mall #1290
Sacramento 95814
323–6225
Fax: 323–6826

Governor's Office of Community Relations
Dir, Los Angeles Regional Office: Eric Bauman
300 S Spring St #16701
Los Angeles 90013
(213) 897–0322
Fax: (213) 897–0319

Office of Criminal Justice Planning
Exec Dir: Frank Grimes
http://www.ocjp.ca.gov
1130 K St #300
Sacramento 95814
324–9100
Fax: 324–9167

Governor's Office of Emergency Services
Dir: Dallas Jones
http://www.oes.ca.gov
2800 Meadowview Rd
Sacramento 95832
262–1816
Fax: 262–2837

Military Department, State of California
Adj Gen: Paul D. Monroe, Jr Major General
9800 Goethe Rd Box 269101
Sacramento 95826–9101
854–3000
Fax: 854–3671

Department of Personnel Administration
Dir: Marty Morgenstern
http://www.dpa.ca.gov
1515 S St No Bldg #400
Sacramento 95814–7243
322–5193
Fax: 322–8376

Office of Planning and Research
Dir: Steven A. Nissen
http://www.opr.ca.gov
Box 3044
Sacramento 95812–3044
322–2318
Fax: 322–3785

State Public Defender
State Pub Def: Lynne S. Coffin
http://www.ospd.ca.gov
221 Main St 10th Flr
San Francisco 94105
(415) 904–5600
Fax: (415) 904–5635

Lieutenant Governor

Cruz M. Bustamante (D)
Elected: 1998
Term Limit: 2006
http://www.ltg.ca.gov
Capitol Building #1114
Sacramento 95814
445–8994
Fax: 323–4998

Attorney General

Bill Lockyer (D)
Elected: 1998
Term Limit: 2006
http://caag.state.ca.us
1300 I St
Sacramento 95814
445–9555

Secretary of State

Bill Jones (R)
Elected: 1994
Term Limit: 2002
http://www.ss.ca.gov
1500 11th St
Sacramento 95814
653–7244
Fax: 653–4620

Treasurer

Philip Angelides (D)
Elected: 1998
Term Limit: 2006
http://www.treasurer.ca.gov
915 Capitol Mall #110
Sacramento 95814
653–2995
Fax: 653–3125

Controller

Kathleen Connell (D)
Elected: 1994
Term Limit: 2002
http://www.sco.ca.gov
300 Capitol Mall 18th Flr
Sacramento 95814
445–3028
Fax: 445–6379

State Superintendent of Public Instruction

Delaine Eastin
Elected: 1994
Term Limit: 2002
http://www.cde.ca.gov/executive/
721 Capitol Mall
Sacramento 95814
657–4766
Fax: 657–4975

Insurance Commissioner

Harry W. Low (D)
Appt: 2000
Term Limit: 2006
http://www.insurance.ca.gov
300 Capitol Mall #1500
Sacramento 95814
492–3500
Fax: 445–5280

Board of Equalization

District 1
Johan Klehs (D)
Elected: 1994
Term Limit: 2002
450 N St #2311 MIC:71
Sacramento 95814
445–4081
Fax: 324–2087

District 2
Dean F. Andal (R)
Elected: 1994
Term Limit: 2002
7540 Shoreline Dr #D
Stockton 95219
(209) 473–6579
Fax: (209) 473–6584

District 3
Claude Parrish (R)
Elected: 1998
Term Limit: 2006
1350 Front St #5022
San Diego 92101
(619) 645–2645
Fax: (619) 645–2647

District 4
John Chiang (D)
Elected: 1998
Term Limit: 2006
660 S Figueroa St #2050
Los Angeles 90017
(213) 239–8506
Fax: (213) 239–8753

Ex-Officio Member
Kathleen Connell (D)
Elected: 1994
Term Limit: 2002
300 Capitol Mall #1850
Sacramento 95814
445–2636
Fax: 322–4404

State Departments

(All numbers 916 area code unless otherwise noted)

Business, Transportation and Housing Agency

Agency Secy: Maria Contreras-Sweet
http://www.bth.ca.gov
980 9th St #2450
Sacramento 95814–3520
323–5400
Fax: 323–5440

Department of Alcoholic Beverage Control
Interim Dir: Manuel Espinoza
http://www.abc.ca.gov
3810 Rosin Ct #150
Sacramento 95834
263–6900
Fax: 263–6912

Department of Corporations
Act Commissioner: William Kenefick
http://www.corp.ca.gov
1515 K St #200
Sacramento 95814
445–7719
Fax: 445–7975

Department of Financial Institutions
Commissioner: Donald R. Meyer
http://www.dfi.ca.gov
111 Pine St #1100
San Francisco 94111–5613
(415) 263–8555
Fax: (415) 989–5310

California Highway Patrol
Commissioner: Dwight "Spike" Helmick
http://www.chp.ca.gov
2555 1st Ave
Sacramento 95818
657–7152
Fax: 657–7324

Department of Housing and Community Development
Dir: Julie I. Bornstein
http://www.hcd.ca.gov
1800 Third St
Sacramento 95814
445–4775
Fax: 324–5107

California Housing Finance Agency
Exec Dir: Theresa A. Parker
http://www.chfa.ca.gov
1121 L St 7th Flr
Sacramento 95814
322–3991
Fax: 322–1464

Department of Managed Health Care
Dir: Daniel Zingale
http://www.dmhc.ca.gov
980 9th St #500
Sacramento 95814–2725
322–2078
Fax: 322–2579

Department of Motor Vehicles
Dir: Steven Gourley
http://www.dmv.ca.gov
2415 1st Ave
Sacramento 95818
657–6518
Fax: 457–7582

Department of Real Estate
Commissioner: Paula Reddish Zinnemann
http://www.dre.ca.gov
2201 Broadway
Sacramento 95818
227–0782
Fax: 227–0777

Office of Traffic Safety
Interim Dir: Teresa Becher
http://www.ots.ca.gov
7000 Franklin Blvd #440
Sacramento 95823–1899
262–0990
Fax: 262–2960

Department of Transportation/Caltrans
Dir: Jeff Morales
http://www.dot.ca.gov
1120 N St #1100
Sacramento 95814
654–5266
Fax: 654–6608

California Environmental Protection Agency

Agency Secy: Winston H. Hickox
http://www.calepa.ca.gov
1001 I St
Sacramento 95814
445–3846
Fax: 445–6401

Integrated Waste Management Board
Chair: Linda Moulton-Patterson
Act Exec Dir: Karin Fish
http://www.ciwmb.ca.gov
8800 Cal Center Dr
Sacramento 95826
255–2200
Fax: 255–2227

Air Resources Board
Chair: Alan C. Lloyd, PhD
Exec Off: Michael P. Kenny
http://www.arb.ca.gov/homepage.htm
1001 I St
Sacramento 95814
322–2990
Fax: 445–5052

Department of Pesticide Regulation
Dir: Paul Helliker
http://www.cdpr.ca.gov
1001 I St
Sacramento 95814–2828
445–4300
Fax: 324–1452

Department of Toxic Substances Control
Dir: Edwin F. Lowry
http://www.dtsc.ca.gov
Box 806
Sacramento 95812–0806
322–0476
Fax: 327–0978

Office of Environmental Health Hazard Assessment
Dir: Joan E. Denton, Ph.D.
http://www.oehha.ca.gov/home.html
1001 I St
Sacramento 95812–4010
324–7572
Fax: 327–1097

Water Resources Control Board
Act Chair: Art Baggett
Act Exec Dir: Ed Anton
http://www.swrcb.ca.gov
1001 I St
Sacramento 95814
341–5250
Fax: 657–1258

Health and Human Services Agency

Agency Secy: Grantland Johnson
http://www.chhs.ca.gov
1600 9th St #460
Sacramento 95814–6404
654–3454
Fax: 654–3343

Department of Aging
Dir: Lynda Terry
http://www.aging.state.ca.us
1600 K St
Sacramento 95814
322–5290
Fax: 324–1903

Department of Alcohol and Drug Programs
Dir: Kathryn P. Jett
http://www.adp.cahwnet.gov
1700 K St 5th Flr
Sacramento 95814–4037
445–1943
Fax: 323–5873

Department of Child Support Services
Dir: Curtis L. Child
http://www.childsup.cahwnet.gov
Box 419064
Sacramento 95741–9064
654–1532

Department of Community Services and Development
Dir: Timothy Dayonot
http://www.csd.ca.gov
700 N 10th St #258
Sacramento 95814
322–2940
Fax: 327–3153

Department of Developmental Services
Dir: Cliff Allenby
http://www.dds.cahwnet.gov
1600 9th St #240 MS:2–13
Sacramento 95814
654–1897
Fax: 654–2167

Emergency Medical Services Authority
Interim Dir: Richard E. Watson
http://www.emsa.ca.gov
1930 9th St
Sacramento 95814
322–4336
Fax: 324–2875

Employment Development Department
Dir: Michael S. Bernick
http://www.edd.cahwnet.gov
800 Capitol Mall #5000
Sacramento 95814
654–8210
Fax: 657–5294

Department of Health Services
Dir: Diana M. Bonta
http://www.dhs.cahwnet.gov
714 P St #1253
Sacramento 95814
657–1425
Fax: 657–1156

Health and Human Services Data Center
Dir: Robert Dell'Agostino
http://www.hwdc.ca.gov
1651 Alhambra Blvd
Sacramento 95816
739–7500
Fax: 739–7933

Managed Risk Medical Insurance Board
Chair: John Geesman
Exec Dir: Sandra Shewry
http://www.mrmib.ca.gov
1000 G St #450
Sacramento 95814
324–4695
Fax: 324–4878

Department of Mental Health
Dir: Stephen W. Mayberg, Ph.D.
http://www.dmh.cahwnet.gov
1600 9th St #151
Sacramento 95814
654–2309
Fax: 654–3198

Department of Rehabilitation
Dir: Catherine Campisi, Ph.D.
http://www.rehab.cahwnet.gov
2000 Evergreen St
Sacramento 95815
263–8987
Fax: 263–7474

Department of Social Services
Dir: Rita L. Saenz
http://www.dss.cahwnet.gov
744 P St #1740
Sacramento 95814
657–3667
Fax: 653–3173

Office of Statewide Health Planning and Development
Dir: David M. Carlisle. M.D, Ph.D.
http://www.oshpd.state.ca.us
1600 9th St #433
Sacramento 95814
654–1606
Fax: 653–1448

Resources Agency

Agency Secy: Mary Nichols
http://ceres.ca.gov/cra
1416 9th St #1311
Sacramento 95814
653–5656
Fax: 653–8102

Department of Boating and Waterways
Interim Dir: Carlton D. Moore
http://www.dbw.ca.gov
2000 Evergreen St #100
Sacramento 95815–3888
263–4326
Fax: 263–0648

California Coastal Commission
Chair: Sara Wan
Exec Dir: Peter Douglas
http://www.coastal.ca.gov
45 Fremont St #2000
San Francisco 94105
(415) 904–5200
Fax: (415) 904–5400

State Coastal Conservancy
Exec Off: William Ahern
http://www.coastalconservancy.ca.gov
1330 Broadway #1100
Oakland 94612–2530
(510) 286–1015
Fax: (510) 286–0470

Colorado River Board of California
Chair: Virgil L. Jones
Exec Dir: Gerald R. Zimmerman
http://crb.water.ca.gov
770 Fairmont Ave #100
Glendale 91203–1035
(818) 543–4676
Fax: (818) 543–4685

California Conservation Corps
Dir: H. Wes Pratt
http://www.ccc.ca.gov
1719 24th St
Sacramento 95816
341–3100
Fax: 323–4989

Department of Conservation
Dir: Darryl W. Young
http://www.consrv.ca.gov
801 K St 24th Flr
Sacramento 95814
322–1080
Fax: 445–0732

Department of Fish and Game
Dir: Robert C. Hight
http://www.dfg.ca.gov
1416 9th St 12th Flr
Sacramento 95814
653–7667
Fax: 653–1856

Forestry and Fire Protection, State Board of
Act Chair: Stan L. Dixon
Exec Off: Christopher P. Rowney
http://www.fire.ca.gov/bof/bof.asp
Box 944246
Sacramento 94244–2460
653–8007
Fax: 653–0989

Department of Forestry and Fire Protection
Dir: Andrea E. Tuttle
http://www.fire.ca.gov
Box 944246
Sacramento 94244–2460
653–5121
Fax: 653–4171

Mining and Geology Board
Chair: Robert Grunwald
Exec Off: John G. Parrish, Ph.D.
http://www.consrv.ca.gov/smgb
801 K St #2436
Sacramento 95814
322–1082
Fax: 445–0738

Department of Parks and Recreation
Dir: Rusty Areias
http://cal-parks.ca.gov
1416 9th St #1405
Sacramento 95814
653–8380
Fax: 657–3903

San Francisco Bay Conservation and Development Commission
Chair: Robert R. Tufts
Exec Dir: Will Travis
http://www.bcdc.ca.gov
50 California St #2600
San Francisco 94111
(415) 352–3600
Fax: (415) 352–3606

Santa Monica Mountains Conservancy
Exec Dir: Joseph T. Edmiston
http://ceres.ca.gov/smmc
5750 Ramirez Canyon Rd
Malibu 90265
(310) 589–3200
Fax: (310) 589–3207

California Tahoe Conservancy
Exec Off: Dennis T. Machida
http://www.tahoecons.ca.gov
2161 Lake Tahoe Blvd #2
South Lake Tahoe 95150
(530) 542–5580
Fax: (530) 542–5591

Department of Water Resources
Dir: Thomas Hannigan
http://www.water.ca.gov
1416 9th St #1115–1
Sacramento 95814
653–5791
Fax: 653–5028

Wildlife Conservation Board (Department of Fish and Game)
Chair: Michael Chrisman
Exec Dir: Al Wright
http://www.dfg.ca.gov/wcb/wcb web page.htm
1807 13th St #103
Sacramento 95814
445–8448
Fax: 323–0280

Office of the Secretary for Education

Secy: Kerry Mazzoni
http://www.ose.ca.gov
1121 L St #600
Sacramento 95814
323–0611
Fax: 323–3753

State and Consumer Services Agency

Agency Secy: Aileen Adams
http://www.scsa.ca.gov
915 Capitol Mall #200
Sacramento 95814
653–2636
Fax: 653–3815

Building Standards Commission, California
Chair: Aileen Adams
Exec Dir: Stan Nishimura
http://www.bsc.ca.gov
2525 Natomas Park Dr #130
Sacramento 95833–2936
263–0916
Fax: 263–0959

Department of Consumer Affairs
Dir: Kathleen Hamilton
http://www.dca.ca.gov
400 R St #300

Sacramento 95814–6200
445–1254
Fax: 445–8796

Fair Employment and Housing Commission
Chair: George Woolverton
455 Golden Gate #14500
San Francisco 94102–3660
(415) 557–2325
Fax: (415) 557–0855

State Fire Marshal
Fire Marshal: John J. Tennant
http://www.fire.ca.gov/FireMarshal/FireMarshal.asp
Box 944246
Sacramento 94244–2460
445–8200
Fax: 445–8509

California Franchise Tax Board
Chair: Dr. Kathleen Connell
Exec Off: Gerald H. Goldberg
http://www.ftb.ca.gov
Box 1468
Sacramento 95812–1468
845–4543
Fax: 845–3191

California Science Center
Exec Dir: Jeffrey N. Rudolph
http://www.casciencectr.org
700 State Dr
Los Angeles 90037
(323) 724–3623
Fax: (213) 744–2034

State Personnel Board
Pres: Ron Alvarado
Exec Off: Walter Vaughn
http://www.spb.ca.gov
801 Capitol Mall
Sacramento 95814
653–1028
Fax: 653–0927

Psychology, Board of
Pres: Martin Greenberg, Ph.D.
Exec Off: Thomas O'Connor
http://www.dca.ca.gov/psych
1422 Howe Ave #22
Sacramento 95825–3200
263–2699
Fax: 263–2697

California Public Employees Retirement System (CalPERS)
Pres: William D. Crist
CEO: James E. Burton
http://www.calpers.ca.gov
400 P St
Sacramento 95814
326–3829
Fax: 326–3410

State Teachers Retirement System
CEO: James Mosman
http://www.calstrs.ca.gov
7667 Folsom Blvd 3rd Flr
Sacramento 95826
229–3700
Fax: 229–3704

Technology, Trade and Commerce Agency

Agency Secy: Lon S. Hatamiya
http://commerce.ca.gov/index.html
801 K St #1918
Sacramento 95814
322–1394
Fax: 323–2887

California Film Commission
Dir: Karen R. Constine
http://film.ca.gov
7080 Hollywood Blvd #900
Hollywood 90028
(323) 860–2960
Fax: (323) 860–2972

Division of International Trade and Investment/World Trade Commission
Dpty Secy: Christopher M. Campana
Regional Mgr: Serge Chemla
http://commerce.ca.gov/international
801 K St #1700
Sacramento 95814–3520
324–5511
Fax: 324–5791

California Division of Tourism/California Travel & Tourism Commission
Exec Dir/Dpty Secy: Caroline Beteta
http://gocalif.ca.gov
801 K St #1600
Sacramento 95814
322–2881
Fax: 322–3402

Small Business Development Center Program
Dir: Kimberley Neri
http://www.commerce.ca.gov/business/small
801 K St #1700
Sacramento 95814
324–5068
Fax: 322–5084

Youth and Adult Correctional Agency

Secy: Robert Presley
http://www.yaca.state.ca.us
1100 11th St #400
Sacramento 95814
323–6001
Fax: 442–2637

Corrections, Board of
Chair: Robert Presley
Exec Dir: Thomas E. McConnell
http://www.bdcorr.ca.gov
600 Bercut Dr
Sacramento 95814
445–5073
Fax: 327–3317

Department of Corrections
Act Dir: Steve Cambra, Jr.
http://www.cdc.state.ca.us
1515 S St
Sacramento 95814
445–7688
Fax: 322–2877

Prison Industry Board
Chair: Steven Cambra, Jr.
Exec Off: Joella M. Fazio
560 E Natoma St
Folsom 95630–2200
358–2677
Fax: 358–1732

Prison Terms, Board of
Chair: David A. Hepburn
Exec Off: Louie DiNinni
http://www.bpt.ca.gov
1515 K St #600
Sacramento 95814
445–4072
Fax: 445–5242

Youth Authority
Dir: Jerry L. Harper
http://www.cya.ca.gov
4241 Williamsbourgh Dr
Sacramento 95823
262–1480
Fax: 262–1483

Youthful Offender Parole Board
Chair: Robert Presley
Administrative Rep: Constance G. Erlich
http://www.yopb.ca.gov
1029 J St #500
Sacramento 95814–2814
322–9800
Fax: 322–8802

California State Senate

(The Capitol address for all members is Sacramento. CA 95814. All area codes 916 unless otherwise noted.)

President
Lt Governor Cruz Bustamante (D)

President pro Tempore
John Burton (D)

Majority Floor Leader
Richard Polanco (D)

Minority Floor Leader
Jim Brulte (R)

Majority Whip
Richard Alarcon (D)

Minority Whip
Ray Haynes (R)

Democratic Caucus Chair
Jack O'Connell

Republican Caucus Chair
Charles Poochigian

(Addresses and staff assignments, current as of January 26, 2001, are subject to change.)

Dick Ackerman (R–33)
Term Limit: 2008
senator.ackerman@sen.ca.gov
Tustin

Richard Alarcon (D–20)
Term Limit: 2006
senator.alarcon@sen.ca.gov
Van Nuys

Deirdre "Dede" Alpert (D–39)
Term Limit: 2004
senator.alpert@sen.ca.gov
San Diego

Jim Battin (R–37)
Term Limit: 2008
jim.battin@sen.ca.gov
Palm Desert

Debra Bowen (D–28)
Term Limit: 2006
senator.bowen@sen.ca.gov
Redondo Beach

Jim Brulte (R–31)
Term Limit: 2004
senator.brulte@sen.ca.gov
Rancho Cucamonga

John Burton (D–3)
Term Limit: 2004
San Francisco

Wes Chesbro (D–2)
Term Limit: 2006
senator.chesbro@sen.ca.gov
Santa Rosa

Jim Costa (D–16)
Term Limit: 2002
senator.costa@sen.ca.gov
Fresno

Joe Dunn (D–34)
Term Limit: 2006
senator.dunn@sen.ca.gov
Garden Grove

Martha M. Escutia (D–30)
Term Limit: 2006
senator.escutia@sen.ca.gov
Norwalk

Liz Figueroa (D–10)
Term Limit: 2006
senator.figueroa@sen.ca.gov
Fremont

Ray Haynes (R–36)
Term Limit: 2002
senator.haynes@sen.ca.gov
Riverside

K. Maurice Johannessen (R–4)
Term Limit: 2002
Redding

Ross Johnson (R–35)
Term Limit: 2004
Irvine

Betty Karnette (D–27)
Term Limit: 2004
senator.karnette@sen.ca.gov
Long Beach

William "Pete" Knight (R–17)
Term Limit: 2004
senator.knight@sen.ca.gov
Palmdal

Sheila Kuehl (D–23)
Term Limit: 2008
Los Angeles

Michael J. Machado (D–5)
Term Limit: 2008
Stockton

Bob Margett (R–29)
Term Limit: 2008
senator.margett@sen.ca.gov
Arcadia

Tom McClintock (R–19)
Term Limit: 2008
tom.mcclintock@sen.ca.gov
Thousand Oaks

Bruce McPherson (R–15)
Term Limit: 2004
senator.mcpherson@sen.ca.gov
Santa Cruz

Dick Monteith (R–12)
Term Limit: 2002
senator.monteith@sen.ca.gov
Modesto

Bill Morrow (R–38)
Term Limit: 2006
senator.morrow@sen.ca.gov
San Juan Capistrano

Kevin Murray (D–26)
Term Limit: 2006
senator.murray@sen.ca.gov
Culver City

Jack O'Connell (D–18)
Term Limit: 2002
senator.oconnell@sen.ca.gov
Santa Barbara

Thomas "Rico" Oller (R–1)
Term Limit: 2008
Roseville

Deborah V. Ortiz (D–6)
Term Limit: 2006
senator.ortiz@sen.ca.gov
Sacramento

Steve Peace (D–40)
Term Limit: 2002
senator.peace@sen.ca.gov
La Mesa

Don Perata (D–9)
Term Limit: 2006
senator.perata@sen.ca.gov
Oakland

Richard Polanco (D–22)
Term Limit: 2002
senator.polanco@sen.ca.gov
Los Angeles

Charles Poochigian (R–14)
Term Limit: 2006
Fresno

Gloria Romero (D–24)
Term Limit: 2008
East Los Angeles

Jack Scott (D–21)
Term Limit: 2008
Pasadena

Byron D. Sher (D–11)
Term Limit: 2004
senator.sher@sen.ca.gov
Redwood City

Nell Soto (D–32)
Term Limit: 2006
Ontario

Jackie Speier (D–8)
Term Limit: 2006
senator.speier@sen.ca.gov
San Mateo

Tom Torlakson (D–7)
Term Limit: 2008
Walnut Creek

John Vasconcellos (D–13)
Term Limit: 2004
senator.vasconcellos@sen.ca.gov
San Jose

Edward Vincent (D–25)
Term Limit: 2008
Inglewood

California State Assembly

(The Capitol address for all members is Sacramento, CA 95814. All area codes 916 unless otherwise noted.)

Speaker
Robert Hertzberg (D)

Speaker pro Tem
Fred Keeley (D)

Assistant Speaker pro Tem
Christine Kehoe (D)

Majority Floor Leader
Kevin Shelley (D)

Assistant Majority Floor Leader
Gill Cedillo (D)

Republican Leader
Dave Cox (R)

Minority Whip
Keith Richman (R)

Democratic Caucus Chair
Dion Aroner

Republican Caucus Chair
Anthony Pescetti

(Addresses and staff assignments, current as of January 26, 2001, are subject to change.)
Vacancy: 65, 49

Sam Aanestad (R–3)
Term Limit: 2004
assemblymember.aanestad@assembly.ca.gov
Grass Valley

Elaine Alquist (D–22)
Term Limit: 2002
assemblywoman.alquist@assembly.ca.gov
Santa Clara

Dion Aroner (D–14)
Term Limit: 2002
dion.aroner@assembly.ca.gov
Berkeley

Roy Ashburn (R–32)
Term Limit: 2002
roy.ashburn@assembly.ca.gov
Bakersfield

Patricia C. Bates (R–73)
Term Limit: 2004
assemblymember.bates@assembly.ca.gov
Laguna Niguel

Mike Briggs (R–29)
Term Limit: 2004
assemblymember.briggs@assembly.ca.gov
Fresno

Thomas M. Calderon (D–58)
Term Limit: 2004
assemblymember.calderon@assembly.ca.gov
Montebello

Bill Campbell (R–71)
Term Limit: 2002
Orange

John Campbell (R–70)
Term Limit: 2006
assemblymember.john.campbell@assembly.ca.gov
Irvine

Joe Canciamilla (D–11)
Term Limit: 2006
assemblymember.canciamilla@ssembly.ca.gov
Martinez

Tony Cardenas (D–39)
Term Limit: 2002
assemblymember.cardenas@assembly.ca.gov
Mission Hills

Dennis A. Cardoza (D–26)
Term Limit: 2002
dennis.cardoza@assembly.ca.gov
Turlock

Gil Cedillo (D–46)
Term Limit: 2004
assemblymember.cedillo@assembly.ca.gov
Los Angeles

Wilma Chan (D–16)
Term Limit: 2006
assemblymember.chan@assembly.ca.gov
Oakland

Edward "Ed" Chavez (D–57)
Term Limit: 2006
assemblymember.chavez@assembly.ca.gov
City of Industry

Dave Cogdill (R–25)
Term Limit: 2006
assemblymember.cogdill@assembly.ca.gov
Modesto

Rebecca Cohn (D–24)
Term Limit: 2006
assemblymember.cohn@assembly.ca.gov
Campbell

Ellen M. Corbett (D–18)
Term Limit: 2004
assemblymember.corbett@assembly.ca.gov
San Leandro

Lou Correa (D–69)
Term Limit: 2004
assemblymember.correa@assembly.ca.gov
Santa Ana

Dave Cox (R–5)
Term Limit: 2004
assemblymember.cox@assembly.ca.gov
Sacramento

Lynn Daucher (R–72)
Term Limit: 2006
assemblymember.daucher@assembly.ca.gov
Brea

Manny Diaz (D–23)
Term Limit: 2006
assemblymember.diaz@assembly.ca.gov
San Jose

Richard Dickerson (R–2)
Term Limit: 2004
assemblymember.dickerson@assembly.ca.gov
Redding

John Dutra (D–20)
Term Limit: 2004
assemblymember.dutra@assembly.ca.gov
Fremont

Marco A. Firebaugh (D–50)
Term Limit: 2004
assemblymember.firebaugh@assembly.ca.gov
Cudahy

Dean Florez (D–30)
Term Limit: 2004
assemblymember.florez@assembly.ca.gov
Bakersfield

Dario J. Frommer (D–43)
Term Limit: 2006
assemblymember.frommer@assembly.ca.gov
Glendale

Jackie Goldberg (D–45)
Term Limit: 2006
assemblymember.goldberg@assembly.ca.gov
Los Angeles

Tom Harman (R–67)
Term Limit: 2006
assemblymember.harman@assembly.ca.gov
Huntington Beach

Sally Havice (D–56)
Term Limit: 2002
assemblymember.havice@assembly.ca.gov
Bellflower

Robert M. Hertzberg (D–40)
Term Limit: 2002
speaker@assembly.ca.gov
Van Nuy

Dennis Hollingsworth (R–66)
Term Limit: 2006
assemblymember.hollingsworth@assembly.ca.gov
Temecula

Jerome E. Horton (D–51)
Term Limit: 2006
assemblymember.horton@assembly.ca.gov
Inglewood

Hannah-Beth Jackson (D–35)
Term Limit: 2004
assemblymember.jackson@assembly.ca.gov
Santa Barbara

Fred Keeley (D–27)
Term Limit: 2002
fred.keeley@assembly.ca.gov
Santa Cruz

Christine Kehoe (D–76)
Term Limit: 2006
assemblymember.kehoe@assembly.ca.gov
San Diego

David G. Key (R–80)
Term Limit: 2006
assemblymember.kelley@assembly.ca.gov
Palm Desert

Paul Koretz (D–42)
Term Limit: 2006
assemblymember.koretz@assembly.ca.gov
West Hollywood

Jay La Suer (R–77)
Term Limit: 2006
assemblymember.lasuer@assembly.ca.gov
La Mesa

Lynne C. Leach (R–15)
Term Limit: 2002
assemblymember.leach@assembly.ca.gov
Walnut Creek

Bill Leonard (R–63)
Term Limit: 2006
assemblymember.leonard@assembly.ca.gov
Rancho Cucamonga

Tim Leslie (R–4)
Term Limit: 2006
assemblymember.leslie@assembly.ca.gov
Sacramento

Carol Liu (D–44)
Term Limit: 2006
assemblymember.liu@assembly.ca.gov
Pasadena

John Longville (D–62)
Term Limit: 2004
assemblymember.longville@assembly.ca.gov
San Bernardino

Alan Lowenthal (D–54)
Term Limit: 2004
alan.lowenthal@assembly.ca.gov
Long Beach

Ken Maddox (R–68)
Term Limit: 2004
ken.maddox@asm.ca.gov
Garden Grove

Abel Maldonado (R–33)
Term Limit: 2004
assemblymember.maldonado@assembly.ca.gov
San Luis Obispo

Barbara Matthews (D–17)
Term Limit: 2006
assemblymember.matthews@assembly.ca.gov
Stockton

Carole Migden (D–13)
Term Limit: 2002
assemblymember.migden@assembly.ca.gov
San Francisco

Dennis Mountjoy (R–59)
Term Limit: 2006
assemblymember.mountjoy@assembly.ca.gov
Arcadia

George Nakano (D–53)
Term Limit: 2004
assemblymember.nakano@assembly.ca.gov
Torrance

Joe Nation (D–6)
Term Limit: 2006
joe.nation@asm.ca.gov
San Rafael

Gloria Negrete McLeod (D–61)
Term Limit: 2006
assemblymember.mcleod@assembly.ca.gov
Montclair

Jenny Oropeza (D–55)
Term Limit: 2006
assemblymember.oropeza@assembly.ca.gov
Carson

Robert Pacheco (R–60)
Term Limit: 2004
robert.pacheco@asm.ca.gov
City of Industry

Rod Pacheco (R–64)
Term Limit: 2002
rod.pacheco@asm.ca.gov
Riverside 97507

Lou Papan (D–19)
Term Limit: 2002
lou.papan@assembly.ca.gov
Millbrae

Fran Pavley (D–41)
Term Limit: 2006
assemblymember.pavley@assembly.ca.gov
Encino

Anthony Pescetti (R–10)
Term Limit: 2004
anthony.pescetti@asm.ca.gov
Sacramento

Sarah Reyes (D–31)
Term Limit: 2004
assemblymember.reyes@assembly.
ca.gov
Fresno 93721

Keith Stuart Richman (R–38)
Term Limit: 2006
assemblymember.richman@assembly.
ca.gov
Granada Hills

George Runner (R–36)
Term Limit: 2002
george.runner@asm.ca.gov
Lancaster

Simon Salinas (D–28)
Term Limit: 2006
assemblymember.salinas@assembly.
ca.gov
Salinas

Kevin Shelley (D–12)
Term Limit: 2002
kevin.shelley@assembly.ca.gov
San Francisco

S. Joseph Simitian (D–21)
Term Limit: 2006
assemblymember.simitian@assembly.
ca.gov
Palo Alto

Darrell Steinberg (D–9)
Term Limit: 2004
assemblymember.steinberg@assembly
.ca.gov
Sacramento

Tony Strickland (R–37)
Term Limit: 2004
assemblymember.stric land@
assembly.ca.gov
Camarillo

Virginia Strom-Martin (D–1)
Term Limit: 2002
virginia.strom-
martin@assembly.ca.gov
Santa Rosa

Helen Thomson (D–8)
Term Limit: 2002
helen.thomson@assembly.ca.gov
Vacaville

Juan Vargas (D–79)
Term Limit: 2006
juan.vargas@asm.ca.gov
National City

Carl Washington (D–52)
Term Limit: 2002
carl.washington@assembly.ca.gov
Compton

Howard Wayne (D–78)
Term Limit: 2002
assemblymember.wayne@assembly.
ca.gov
San Diego

Herb Wesson (D–47)
Term Limit: 2004
assemblymember.wesson@assembly.
ca.gov
Los Angeles

Patricia Wiggins (D–7)
Term Limit: 2004
assemblymember.wiggins@assembly
ca.gov
Santa Rosa

Roderick Wright (D–48)
Term Limit: 2002
assemblymember.wright@assembly.
ca.gov
Los Angeles

Mark Wyland (R–74)
Term Limit: 2006
assemblymember.wyland@assembly.
ca.gov
Vista

Phil Wyman (R–34)
Term Limit: 2006
assemblymember.wyman@assembly.
ca.gov
Tehachapi

Charlene Zettel (R–75)
Term Limit: 2004
assemblymember.zettel@assembly.
ca.gov
Poway

APPENDIX C

Useful Websites

Association of Bay Area Governments
www.abag.ca.gov

Audubon California (environmental issues)
www.audubon-ca.org

Border Region Information
www.borderecoweb.sdsu.edu

California Court system
www.courtinfo.ca.gov

California Futures Network (growth/ development issues)
www.calfutures.org

California Geographical Survey
http://goegodata.csun.edu/

California Government Agency and Commission List
www.ganymede.org/agencies.html

California Higher Education Policy Center
www.policy center.org

California Historical Society
www.calhist.org

California Law References
www.leginfo.ca.gov/calaw.html

California Research Bureau
www.library.ca.gov

California Secretary of State
www.ss.ca.gov

California State Assembly
www.assembly.ca.gov

California State Association of Counties
www.csac.counties.org

California State Home Page
www.ca.gov

California State Senate
www.senate.ca.gov

California State University System
www.ca.gov/s/learning/csu.html

Center for California Studies
www.csus.edu/calst/index.html

Center for Responsive Politics (tracking money in campaigns)
www.opensecrets.org

Chicano/Latino Net
www.clnet.ucr.edu

Cities Counties Schools
www.ccspartnership.org

Community College Chancellor's Office
www.cccco.edu

Community College League of California
www.ccleague.org

Institute for Governmental Studies UC Berkeley
www.igs.berkeley.edu:8880

League of California Cities
www.cacities.org

League of Women Voters of California
www.ca.lwv.org

Public Policy Institute of California
www.ppic.org

Search Bills in the California Legislature
www.sen.ca.gov/www/leginfo/SearchText.html

Southern California Association of Governments (SCAG)
www.scg.ca.gov

U.S. Census Data
www.census.gov

University of California System
www.ca.gov/s/learning/uc.html

APPENDIX D

Getting in Touch with Your Elected Officials: A Simple Guide

Since every Californian is represented by multiple elected officials, it can be confusing to find the one you need. Each of us has two U.S. Senators, one member of Congress, one state Senator, one Assembly member, as well as eight constitutional officers (including the governor). Then, at the local level, you have a county supervisor, a city council representative (unless you live in an unincorporated area), and numerous school board and community college board representatives.

How Can You Find the Person You Need?

1. Analyze the situation. Do you need a local, state, or federal response? If you wish to express your views on legislation, make sure you know whether it is in Washington, D.C., Sacramento, or your city hall. Get the bill number and the author's name.
2. If you need a state official, check Appendix B and skim the list to see if your city or community is listed. All state legislators receive mail at: State Capitol, Sacramento, CA 95814. Due to term limits, the list changes frequently. You can use the Web or a local phone book to verify the names of your current representatives.
3. Use your local telephone directory to find out who represents you. Almost all phone books now have listings for "GOVERNMENT OFFICIALS," for all three levels of government.
4. Use the Web to find your elected officials. Go to these as needed:
   www.assembly.ca.gov
   www.senate.ca.gov
   www.house.gov/writerep/
   http://thomas.loc.gov/
5. Verify the name and address by phoning the local office of the elected official. Once you know the name and address, follow these steps:
   1. Address your letter to "Honorable Mr. or Ms. XXX" and use the proper address.
   2. Use your own words to briefly describe your problem, concern, or question. If you are writing to express your views about specific legislation,

refer to the bill number and the author's name. Be brief and constructive in your comments. Explain your reasons for your views on the issue.

3. Be sure to include your signature, your printed name, and your full address. Most elected officials will respond to your letter—however, this may take several months.

Remember, most elected officials only get feedback from organized interest groups and their members. Your individual letter is often considered as having the impact of hundreds of people's views. Your letter can make a difference!

Glossary

Acculturate The process by which immigrants learn their new culture's language, customs, and traditions.

Amend To change a document such as a bill.

Assimilation The process by which a new group learns the rules of the more established group and adapts its customs.

At-large In contrast to district elections, a method of electing members of a city council or other legislative body by voters in the entire governmental unit.

Ballot initiative See *Initiative.*

Ballot status Appearing on the ballot, such as a political party.

Baseline budget A budget based on the previous year's budget rather than a "zero-based" budget which requires all programs to justify their existence.

Blanket primary A primary in which all candidates from every party are listed together.

Bond issues Interest-bearing government securities, authorized at the state or local level by voter approval of a ballot proposition, by which money is borrowed for prison construction or some other purpose.

Bracero Legal temporary immigrant worker, usually brought from Mexico to work in agriculture.

Challenger In politics, a person who runs against an incumbent.

Civil liberties Protected types of behavior such as freedom of speech or religion, which governments are prohibited from taking away.

Civil rights Legally imposed obligations, such as the right to equal protection of the laws or reasonable bail, that governments owe to individuals.

Civil service system A set of procedures for hiring government employees on the basis of merit, usually demonstrated by examination, and protecting them against unjust firing.

Class gap An increasing gap in resources between the wealthiest and the poorest people.

Closed primary The kind of primary used in California and most other states, in which only voters registered as members of a political party can vote for the nomination (selection) of that party's candidates.

Conference committee A temporary committee appointed to resolve differences between the Senate and Assembly versions of a bill.

Conservative A political philosophy which favors smaller government, lower taxes, fewer public services, and a "laissez-faire" (let them do as they please) approach to business.

Constitutional offices The executive officials that the state constitution requires must be elected by the voters.

Council-manager A form of city government in which the elected city council, with legislative authority, appoints, and can fire, a city manager to whom the various executive departments are responsible.

County committee Also known as "county central committee"; a group of elected party activists within each county.

Decline to state A voter's registration status when he or she does not wish to affiliate with any political party.

Defendant In criminal cases, the person accused of a crime, or, in a civil matter, an individual business or government entity being sued.

Deindustrialization Loss of industries and thus jobs, often seen as the result of automation, computerization, and the ability of capital to move anywhere where labor is cheaper and profits are higher.

Demilititarization A reduction in military and defense-related industries, with resulting losses in jobs.

Demographic shift Noticeable changes in population data, including numbers of people, sizes of ethnic groups, etc.

Deregulation When government permits private enterprise to operate with reduced government oversight. Sometimes linked to "free market" economic theories.

Devolution When the federal government gives or returns powers to the states or local governments.

Direct Democracy The reforms of the Progressive movement which enable voters to make laws directly, amend the state constitution, recall officials, or repeal laws passed by elected representatives.

District elections When a city, school district, or other governmental unit is divided into geographic districts, each of which has a representative elected by the voters in that district.

Electoral votes The number of votes a state may cast in electing the President and Vice President of the United States, computed by adding the number of its U.S. Senators (two) to the number of Representatives (52 for California as of 1990).

Electorate Those who vote.

Ethnocentrism A belief that one ethnic or cultural group is superior to others.

Executive clemency The governor's power to lighten criminal sentences imposed by the courts by pardons, which cancel them; commutations, which reduce them; or reprieves, which postpone them. Amnesties are pardons for an entire group.

Ex-officio A nonvoting member of a governmental body.

Federalism A political system in which the national and state systems have some powers independent of each other.

Felonies The most serious crimes, including murder, rape, arson, etc.

Franchise In politics, the right to vote.

Gerrymandered A district whose boundaries have been drawn by a legislature to favor the election of a particular group, individual, or candidate of the dominant political party.

Get out the Vote (GOTV) Campaign strategy including phone calls, rides to the polls, free donuts, etc.

Grassroots Pertaining to actions, movements, or organizations of a political nature that rely chiefly on the mass involvement of ordinary citizens.

Gubernatorial Pertaining to the office of governor.

Homophobia Fear and/or hatred of homosexuals.

Image making Creating a positive impression about a candidate through the use of public relations methods and mass media.

Immigrant bashing The blaming of immigrants, whether legal or undocumented, for social problems.

Incumbent Person currently in office.

Indictment Formal accusation of criminal behavior by a grand jury, sometimes used to bring defendants to trial.

Inflation(ary) A situation in which prices increase rapidly.

Infractions Minor criminal offenses, such as jaywalking.

Infrastructure The tangible components which allow society to function: bridges, roads, water systems, sewage systems, etc.

Initiative The process by which citizens can propose a state or local law or amendment to the state constitution by signing a formal petition asking that it be submitted as a ballot proposition for voter approval.

Issue-oriented organizations Groups concerned primarily with political issues, such as abortion, civil rights, medical care, etc., as opposed to groups interested in electing specific candidates.

Item veto Sometimes called the line-item veto, the authority of the governor to reduce or eliminate money appropriated by the legislature for a specific purpose while signing the remaining provisions of the bill into law.

Left-wing A political approach which tends to value social equality and government intervention to achieve it rather than "laissez-faire" (let them do as they please).

Liberal A political philosophy which supports active government involvement in creating a more just society and which supports individual freedoms in personal matters.

Lobbying The attempt to influence government policy, usually on behalf of an interest group.

Majority More than 50 percent.

Mandates Requirements; i.e., a federal mandate may require states to take a particular action.

Manifest destiny The justification of U.S. territorial expansion based on the mystical assumption that it was the clear fate of the nation to acquire at least all land between the Atlantic and Pacific Oceans.

Marginal Uncertain, on the edge; a district, in contrast to the more numerous "safe" ones, in which the election outcome is uncertain because neither party has an overwhelming advantage in registered voters.

Mayor-council The traditional form of city government based on a separation of powers between a mayor with executive authority and a council with legislative authority, both elected by the voters.

Mestizo Of mixed race, particularly Spanish European and pre-Columbian Indian heritage.

Minimalist That which is limited to its simplest or most essential elements; politically, the usually conservative belief that government should do very little.

Misdemeanors An intermediate level of crime, less damaging to persons or property than a felony.

Monocultural electorate A term which describes the trend toward a largely white electorate, in contrast to a largely nonwhite population at large.

Naturalization The process of becoming a U.S. citizen.

Nonpartisan Elections, such as those of judges, school board members, and city and county officials in California, in which the party affiliation of the candidates does not appear on the ballot.

Office-block ballot To discourage straight-ticket party voting, the arrangement of candidates' names according to the office for which they are running rather than their party affiliations.

Ordinance A law passed by a city or county.

Out of the closet A gay male or lesbian who is open about his or her sexual orientation.

Override When the legislative body votes again on a bill vetoed by the executive, and overcomes the veto by a two-thirds majority so that the bill becomes law without the executive's approval.

Partisan Elections, such as those of national and most state officials, in which the party affiliation of the candidates appears on the ballot; any action or attitude reflecting strong loyalty to a party or political faction.

Party affiliation An individual's choice of a party when registering to vote; may or may not include any activity in that party.

Plaintiff The person bringing suit in a civil case.

Plea bargain Negotiations in a criminal case designed to get the defendant to plead guilty if the prosecution reduces the seriousness of the charge or reduces the sentence.

Plurality The most votes.

Polarization A sharp division between groups, e.g., the increasing differences in views between conservative Republicans and liberal Democrats.

Political Action Committee (PAC) An organization, usually formed by an interest group or corporation, designed to solicit money from individuals to be used for campaign contributions to candidates endorsed by the group.

President Pro Tem The leader of the state Senate, elected by the membership.

Pressure groups Also known as interest groups; organizations which lobby politicians to achieve their political and economic aims.

Private sector Refers to all business and other activities that are not sponsored directly by government; however, much of the American private sector is subsidized through government funds.

Privatization Any effort to cut back government and substitute private sector activity, e.g., firing public janitors and "contracting out" to a private profit-seeking janitorial service.

Progressive movement The growing demand in the early part of the century for such democratic reforms as the initiative and referendum.

Propositions Items on the ballot which require a "yes" or "no" vote, including initiatives, referenda, recalls, bond issues, etc.

Public sector Those activities and agencies sponsored by government and paid for from tax revenues.

Recall A Progressive-era reform that permits the voters, by petition, to call a special election to remove an offical from office before the next regularly scheduled election.

Recession A period during which the economy slows down, including fewer jobs, higher unemployment, lower consumption, and reduced tax revenues.

Redbaiting During the Cold War, the effort to discredit a person by implying that he or she was a Communist ("red").

Redistricting Redrawing the boundaries of election districts; required after each Census to keep district populations as nearly equal as possible.

Referendum The type of ballot proposition which allows voters to repeal or revoke laws passed by the legislature.

Regressive In reference to taxation, indicates that, in proportion to their incomes, the poor are taxed more than the rich.

Runoff election An election held when no candidate in a nonpartisan primary receives a majority; the two top candidates enter a "runoff" so that the final winner is elected by a majority vote.

Safe districts Election districts in which one party, through gerrymandering, is nearly guaranteed victory at the polls.

Scapegoating The process of blaming a social/ethnic group for society's problems.

Speaker of the Assembly The presiding officer and most powerful member of the Assembly, elected by the membership.

Special district Local units of government which perform a service that no city or county provides, and which may encompass an area larger than any one city or county, and which have their own governing body, either appointed or elected.

Standing committee Permanent committees of the California Senate and Assembly organized around policy subjects, to which every bill is referred and in which most of the work of legislation occurs.

States' rights The concept that the fifty states must have greater autonomy in relation to the federal government.

Statutes Laws that are in government code books and are not part of an actual constitution or charter.

Swing vote(r)s Describes those whose votes are not predictable and who can be swayed to support candidates or issues.

Target audience A select group of voters who receive political mailings with messages aimed at winning their support.

Tax assessment In reference to property taxes, the amount which must be paid; it is based on the property's assessed value.

Term limits A rule which permits a politician only a limited number of opportunities to run for the same office. Term limits exist at the state level and in some cities in California.

Two-tier society A society in which there is a small affluent upper class, and a large class of impoverished people, including the working poor and the underclass, and a small middle class.

Underclass Those long-term impoverished persons who survive through government assistance, charity, or criminal activity. They should not be confused with the "working poor," although income levels may be similar.

Unincorporated areas That territory outside the boundaries of incorporated cities whose residents receive nearly all municipal services from county government.

Unitary In contrast to a federal system, one in which the county and other regional or local governments have only the powers the state gives to them.

Upset An election in which the outcome is a surprise to political observers.

User fees Fees for recreational facilities and other public services by which those who use the services pay at least part of the costs of providing the services.

Veto The return of a bill by the chief executive to the legislative body which passed it, unsigned, thereby killing it unless the legislature overrides the veto.

White flight The process by which whites move away from areas as ethnic minorities begin to move in.

Bibliography

Baldassare, Mark, *California in the New Millenium: The Changing Social and Political Landscape,* University of California Press, 2000.

Bonacich, Edna, and Appelbaum, Richard, *Behind the Label: Inequality in the Los Angeles Apparel Industry,* University of California Press, 2000.

Brechin, Gray, *Imperial San Francisco: Urban Power, Earthly Ruin,* University of California Press, 1999.

Chan, Sucheng, and Spencer Olin, *Major Problems in California History,* Houghton Mifflin, 1997.

Clark, Thurston, *California Fault: Searching for the Spirit of a State Along the San Andreas,* Ballantine Books, 1996.

Collier, Michael, *A Land in Motion: California's San Andreas Fault,* University of California Press, 1999.

DeLeon, Richard, *Left Coast City: Progressive Politics in San Francisco, 1975–1991,* University Press of Kansas, 1991.

Deverell, William, and Sitton, Tom, *California Progressivism Revisited,* University of California Press, 1994.

Fradkin, Philip, *The Seven States of California: A Natural and Human History,* University of California Press, 1999.

Fulton, William, *The Reluctant Metropolis: The Politics of Urban Growth in Los Angeles,* Solano Press Books, 1997.

Glantz, Stanton A., and Balbach, Edith, *Tobacco War: Inside the California Battle,* University of California Press, 2000.

Gordon, Bernard, *Hollywood Exile or How I learned to Love the Blacklist,* University of Texas Press, 2000.

Gumprecht, Blake, *The Los Angeles River: Its Life, Death and Possible Rebirth,* Johns Hopkins University Press, 1999.

Gutierrez, Ramon A., and Orsi, Richard, *Contested Eden: California Before the Gold Rush,* University of California Press, 1998.

Haslam, Gerald, *Workin' Man Blues: Country Music in California,* University of California Press, 1999.

Hise, Greg, and William Deverell, *Eden by Design: The 1930 Olmsted-Bartholomew Plan for the Los Angeles Region,* University of California Press, 2000.

King, Rob, M. Poster, and S. Olin, *Postsuburban California: The Transformation of Orange County Since World War II,* University of California Press, 1991.

Lamare, James W., *California Politics: Economics, Power and Policy,* West Books, 1994).

McClung, William Alexander, *Landscapes of Desire: Anglo Mythologies of Los Angeles*, University of California Press, 2000.

Merchant, Carolyn, *Green Versus Gold: Sources in California's Environmental History*, Island Press, 1998.

Mulholland, Catherine, *William Mulholland and the Rise of Los Angeles*, University of California Press, 2000.

Pincetl, Stephanie, *Transforming California: A Political History of Land Use and Development*, Johns Hopkins University Press, 1999.

Rodriguez, Richard, *Days of Obligation: An Argument with My Mexican Father*, Viking Press, 1992.

Saito, Leland, *Race and Politics: Asian Americans, Latinos and Whites in a Los Angeles Suburb*, University of Illinois Press, 1998.

Schrag, Peter, *Paradise Lost: California's Experience, America's Future*, University of California Press, 1998.

Schwartz, Stephen, *From West to East: California and the Making of the American Mind*, Free Press, 1998.

Yung, Judy, *Unbound Voices: A Documentary History of Chinese Women in San Francisco*, University of California Press, 1999.

Index

Note: entries followed by a small *f* refer to figures, and by a small *t* refer to tables.